GW00685209

your first **channel** CROSSING

ADLARD COLES NAUTICAL

B L O O M S B U R Y

LONDON · NEW DELHI · NEW YORK · SYDNEY

Published by Adlard Coles Nautical
an imprint of Bloomsbury Publishing Plc
50 Bedford Square, London WC1B 3DP
www.adlardcoles.com

Copyright © Andy Du Port 2013

First published by Adlard Coles Nautical in 2013

ISBN 978-1-4081-0012-7
ePub 978-1-4081-5908-8
ePDF 978-1-4081-5907-1

All rights reserved. No part of this publication may be reproduced in any form or by any means – graphic, electronic or mechanical, including photocopying, recording, taping or information storage and retrieval systems – without the prior permission in writing of the publishers.

The right of the author to be identified as the author of this work has been asserted by him in accordance with the Copyright, Designs and Patents Act, 1988.

A CIP catalogue record for this book is available from the British Library.

This book is produced using paper that is made from wood grown in managed, sustainable forests. It is natural, renewable and recyclable. The logging and manufacturing processes conform to the environmental regulations of the country of origin.

Typeset in 11 pt UEWGrotesk Light by James Watson
Printed and bound by Zrinski, Croatia

Note: while all reasonable care has been taken in the publication of this book, the publisher takes no responsibility for the use of the methods or products described in the book.

ANDY DU PORT

your first **channel** CROSSING

contents

introduction

The best thing I know between France and England is the sea.
Douglas William Jerrold

So, you have been sailing for some time and consider yourself to be a competent and confident yachtsman in your local waters? But you haven't yet had the opportunity to sail off across the horizon to explore the delights of foreign shores? Perhaps you are rather daunted by the prospect of such a long passage and worried that you won't be able to make yourself understood when you arrive. If so, this book is for you. It will take you through the whole process of preparation, planning and making the crossing, not by a series of checklists and instructions, but rather by discussion of the salient issues which a skipper must consider, whether he or she is making the trip for the first time or has been crossing the English Channel regularly for years.

Almost all of what follows is equally applicable to sailing yachts and motor cruisers. Any advice particular to power craft is shown in tinted boxes.

There are, incidentally, many opinions on the correct term for a 'power-driven leisure craft'. I have tried to include as many as possible, but they should all be taken to mean the same thing: any leisure craft which relies entirely on an engine for propulsion.

You will also find some advice on regulations and procedures on arrival in France, and a short list of useful French words to get you started. But don't worry if your French is virtually non-existent: there will usually be someone in the harbour or marina office who speaks reasonable English.

A certain level of knowledge and expertise has been assumed – about that of an RYA Day Skipper – but I make no apology for going into some fundamental aspects of navigation, collision avoidance and safety. Whatever your experience, it never does any harm to be reminded of the basics. A good skipper or navigator will always welcome a check on his/her work, and will never be too proud to ask for a second opinion when in doubt.

Although the principles of seamanship and navigation hold true for all craft, large and small, the differences between power-driven vessels and sailing yachts are well recognised and it is appreciated that a motorboat may have a cruising speed of 15–20 knots, while a sailing yacht travels relatively slowly (we use an average speed of about 5½ knots throughout this book). Wind direction and tidal streams, in particular, become major factors in planning and executing a passage under sail; they will not affect a power craft to the same extent.

This doesn't mean that tidal streams may be ignored when passage making in a motor yacht; far from it. However, where only a small alteration of course may be sufficient to counter the stream when travelling at 20 knots, a 5-knot sailing boat might have difficulty in making any progress at all in the same conditions.

Similarly, the wind direction may not be of special concern, but its strength, and therefore the sea state, may affect a fast motorboat far more than a sailing yacht.

We will focus on a typical crossing from the Solent to Cherbourg, but the principles are exactly the same for any 12–18 hour passage, much of which will be out of sight of land. When it comes to selecting a suitable weather window, preparing the boat and crew, drawing up and conducting the navigational plan and, crucially, making a safe landfall and entry into your chosen port, it doesn't matter whether you are sailing from Yarmouth to Cherbourg, Ramsgate to Ostend or Holyhead to Dún Laoghaire.

For the same passage a motor cruiser may take just 3–4 hours, but the motion and noise at 20 knots will make activities such as preparing food or plotting a position on the chart much more difficult, and this needs to be taken into account in the early planning stages.

All the advice in this book is based on the experience of over a hundred Channel crossings, many before the days when yachts were routinely fitted with radar, GPS, AIS or even VHF radios. In those days it was not uncommon to ask a passing merchant ship (by flashing light) for a position, and it was good practice to aim 5 miles or so to one side of your destination so you knew which way to turn when sighting land in order to make landfall in your intended port. The only means of calling for help when no other vessels were in sight was by firing off flares.

GPS and all the other electronic gizmos, which we now take for granted, have revolutionised many aspects of life at sea. Navigation has become much simpler and more precise; radar and AIS are both invaluable aids in avoiding collisions. However, wind, weather and rough seas still have to be contended with, and a well-developed sense of seamanship, backed up with a certain level of expertise and hands-on experience, is still essential.

Nowadays in the Solent or English Channel, overhearing a PAN PAN or MAYDAY call, even in relatively benign weather, is quite common. Before VHF radios were widely fitted (and accepting that there were not as many leisure craft at sea), I am not aware that there were any fewer 'emergencies' among the sailing fraternity. We just had to prepare thoroughly, sort out any problems and look after ourselves. Indeed, anyone who sets off without thorough preparation is asking for trouble. At worst you could place your boat and crew in danger; at best you will have a grumpy crew who have missed out on a good meal ashore because their skipper got the tides wrong.

North Brittany coast

In the UK we are mercifully free from requirements to hold any qualifications before going to sea in small craft, leaving us to choose which courses and qualifications best meet our needs. We have a good safety record compared with many other EU countries which do have compulsory qualifications. I firmly believe it is in our interests to keep it that way by taking all reasonable precautions to ensure the safety of ourselves, our crew and our boats.

All aspects of making the passage across the Channel are explained and discussed here: forward planning, preparation, setting off, the crossing itself, arrival and, critically, getting home again. There are notes on selected ports from Falmouth to Dover and from L'Aber Wrac'h to Calais. Most sailing directions, pilots and almanacs describe the entry to a port or harbour, whereas in this book we also look at the *departure* from UK ports. And in Chapter 9 you will find some reminders about procedures in an emergency.

Crossing the English Channel is not difficult. Although the distances involved may appear intimidating, they need to be kept in perspective: in a favourable breeze, the passage from Nab Tower to Cherbourg takes about 12 hours, and is almost exactly the same distance as Portsmouth to Poole and back. It is well within the capabilities of any competent sailor in a sound and well-equipped boat. It should present a bit of a challenge, and be instructive, satisfying and, above all else, fun. Why else do we go sailing?

Frequent references are made throughout the book to *Reeds Nautical Almanac*, the 'Yachtsman's Bible' (referred to simply as *Reeds*), where a plethora of information may be found covering all aspects of passage planning and much more. The *Reeds Channel Almanac*, covering both sides of the English Channel and the Channel Islands, has all the same navigational content but the sections on reference data, regulations, navigation, tides, communications, weather, safety and first aid are much abridged.

The north coast of France is a wonderfully relaxed and friendly cruising ground with countless places to explore, and many good beaches, bars and restaurants. And it's only a day's sail away.

Dover, Eastern Arm

forward planning

Planning is an unnatural process; it is much more fun to do something. The nicest thing about not planning is that failure comes as a complete surprise rather than being preceded by a period of worry and depression.
Sir John Harvey-Jones

Wind, weather and sea state

These are probably uppermost in your mind when planning any sailing trip. The wind is obviously a major consideration for sailing yachts: too much will put considerable strain on you, your crew and your boat; too little and you are faced with a late arrival or a tedious passage under power. But actually the sea state is even more critical. Any well-found yacht should be able to cope with a gale in sheltered waters, and sailing in such conditions can be fun, exhilarating and perfectly safe. Offshore, the same wind, particularly if it has been blowing for some time, will raise potentially dangerous seas for small craft. Force 6 is often said to be a 'yachtsman's gale', and force 5 is probably as much as most of us would wish to cope with on a longish passage, especially if beating into it. Remember that the forecast wind is the average strength; you can reasonably expect gusts of at least one force higher.

Sea state is even more of a consideration in a motor yacht. Moderately rough seas will make for a very uncomfortable trip or will force you to slow down, thus considerably extending the time on passage. Normally simple tasks, such as making a cup of tea, all become much harder. Plugging into a rough sea will also use much more fuel, and this must be allowed for during the planning process.

Wind direction

This is fundamental. A good breeze on the beam may result in some pleasant and fast sailing, but the same wind on the nose will become a trial of strength, not to mention the extra time needed to complete the passage. When beating into the wind you will cover at least one and a half times the direct distance to reach your destination, and the time taken will be even greater as the waves will also reduce your speed through the water. However, although a downwind sail across the Channel in a brisk northerly wind may sound attractive, bear in mind that it will be blowing onshore at the other end. This is not a problem in moderate weather or for somewhere like Cherbourg with its wide, deep entrances, but it may present difficult or even dangerous conditions at other harbours in the area. A stiff north-easterly, for example, will mean a very uncomfortable stay in Alderney. On the other hand, a beat from the UK against a southerly force 4 will generally mean calmer seas and an offshore wind as you close the coast.

While the wind is reasonably predictable and usually well forecast, the sea state depends not only on the strength of the wind but also its direction and fetch – the unobstructed distance directly upwind. So while a gale in the Solent will rarely produce threatening seas, it will be a very different story in the middle of the English Channel. Wind waves take time to calm down, and a nasty sea will still be running for 24 hours or so after a prolonged westerly gale even if the actual wind has moderated to a gentle force 3–4.

TELLTALE

The relationships between wind speed, direction and sea state were dramatically brought home to me when I was a young and relatively inexperienced skipper of one of the ex-German 'windfall' yachts in the

Approaching Portsmouth from the south east

1970s. We were leaving St Peter Port on a grey morning to make our way back to Dartmouth. Apart from the mate, my crew were all under training and for several of them this was their first trip across the Channel and back. As we departed there was quite a brisk tidal stream setting north through the Little Russel, and the forecast was for north easterly winds at about force 5. At the time, it was blowing force 4 from the north. My plan was to motor up the Little Russel with the stream but against the wind then hoist the sails and bear away for the Dart. The first clue that this might not be the best plan was the sight of other yachts – who we knew were also heading for the West Country – turning south out of the harbour to make passage via Les Hanois on the south west tip of Guernsey. The second clue was given by a glance to the north at the fairly obvious overfalls in the vicinity of Platte beacon. Neither clue registered strongly in my mind and, undaunted, we set off.

It did not take long for me to realise my mistake as we shipped the first standing wave over the foredeck. In those days, although we were issued with lifejackets and harnesses, they were awkward, bulky pieces of equipment, and we rarely wore them. The next wave was much the same, but the third was huge and swept with surprising force down the entire length of the 50-foot yacht. Having been at the helm, I found myself half drowned, clinging to the pushpit and looking astern where I assumed at least one of the crew must be floating helplessly as the stream rushed the boat northwards past Roustel beacon. A moment of panic as I wondered what the naval authorities would have to say to a skipper who lost half his crew overboard, before a headcount established that everyone was still on board – wet, frightened but safe. A few minutes later we were clear of the overfalls and set course to leave Platte Fougère to port and then to Dartmouth where we arrived some 10 hours later.

To say that I learnt much from this experience is an understatement. Ever since, I have had the utmost respect for wind-over-tide situations. Also, I am no longer young enough to know everything. Now, when I see a bunch of yachts taking a particular course of action which differs from my plan (even though we are all bound for the same destination), I ask myself why I am clearly in the minority. Don't be tempted to follow the herd blindly, but at least ask the right question!

Weather forecasts

We are spoilt for choice, but weather forecasts don't always tell the same story. The English Channel is well served by the Met Office shipping and inshore forecasts, broadcast by the BBC on Radio 4 and on VHF by the Maritime Rescue Co-ordination Centres (MRCC) at Dover, Lee-on-the-Solent, Portland, Brixham and Falmouth. Details of the broadcast times and the sea areas covered can be found in *Reeds* or on the Maritime and Coastguard Agency (MCA) website. Be careful to note whether the times are shown in UTC (GMT) or in local time (LT). For the midday and early evening BBC Radio 4 broadcasts (on 198kHz) you will need a radio capable of receiving long wave (LW) transmissions. The inshore forecast is more detailed but is only valid for up to 12 miles off the UK coast.

If you have access to the internet, the options are almost endless. Just google 'weather forecast' and you will see what I mean. The Met Office website (*www.metoffice.gov.uk/weather/marine*) shows the shipping and inshore forecasts, and also surface pressure charts for the next three days. Other websites show more or less detail, but be careful: more detail does not necessarily mean more accuracy. It is a common misconception that a weather chart covered with computer-generated little arrows of various colours somehow tells a more reliable story. Similarly, a forecast showing a wind speed of 19 knots (or MPH – check which) is no more accurate than one showing a round 20 knots. What's a knot between friends? They both mean 'force 5'. Any forecast is compiled using relatively limited raw data and relies on the skill and judgement of the forecaster.

No forecast is able to predict sea state with any accuracy. Wind speed, its direction and fetch all affect sea state, which can vary enormously within a few miles. You must judge how rough it is likely to be by looking at the chart as well as listening to the forecast.

Beware of falling into the trap of thinking that a down-sea passage is going to be safer and more comfortable than ploughing into the waves. This may be the case in many sailing yachts, but holding a course in a power craft is almost invariably more difficult, and 'corkscrewing' down sea can be very uncomfortable indeed. Not only that, but exhaust fumes will be blown into the wheelhouse, causing potential problems for even the strongest of stomachs.

Most of us can look out of the window and make a fair judgement about what the weather is up to, but few of us are able to predict the weather for more than a few hours ahead without the assistance of specialised instruments or an 'official' forecast. Trust your instincts and observations to an extent, but just because it looks good doesn't mean it's going to stay that way. For your first Channel crossing you really do not want the additional worry of marginal weather. Far better to amend your plans early rather than set out, only to run for home with your tail between your legs when the going gets tough or mutiny threatens. If your time is limited, look far enough ahead to have a good chance of a safe return trip. Being caught out in ugly weather because you have to be back in the office on Monday morning may be bad luck but is more likely to be a sign of poor planning or recklessness. The cost of a ferry or air fare to get you home is a small price to pay for safety. We look at weather in rather more detail in Chapter 5.

Day or night?

Your first instinct may be to make your first cross-Channel passage in daylight: you and your crew will be more alert during your natural periods of wakefulness; your crew may find the passage more interesting (and possibly less daunting); setting off after an early breakfast and arriving for supper makes for a good day's sailing programme; unless you have experience of sailing at night the boat may be easier to manage by day; you may feel that collision avoidance is simpler; and it may seem that navigation is more straightforward. Night passages will be discussed later, but let's look at some of these issues now.

The paragraph above is, of course, just as applicable to motorboats. However, the chances of hitting flotsam are much higher at night – discarded fishing nets are a significant hazard for power vessels. Whereas a semi-submerged baulk of timber may be shouldered aside by a 5-knot yacht, it could cause considerable damage to a 20-knot motorboat. For this reason alone, I would be very wary of making this passage under power at night.

First, fixing your position as you approach an unfamiliar coast can be much easier when lighthouses are still flashing. A light showing a specified sequence of flashes (its characteristics) is immediately identifiable: what looks like a grey lighthouse on a grey morning may turn out to be the chimney of a power station several miles away. GPS, radar and chart plotters have to some extent overcome this, but all electronics are vulnerable to getting wet or accidental damage, and you must be prepared and able to navigate from basic principles if necessary.

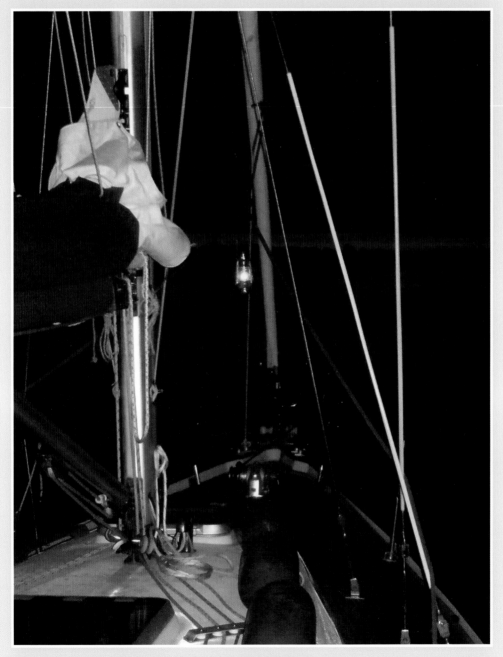

At anchor for the night, before the morning's crossing

Second, collision avoidance is not necessarily more difficult at night. Indeed, it is often easier to determine another ship's aspect by her lights than by the hazy outline of her hull. Generally, alterations of a ship's course are also easier to detect by changes in the relative positions of her navigation lights. Without doubt, though, estimating the ranges of other ships at night is not straightforward. A supertanker at 10 miles might seem to be at the same range as a coaster at half the distance.

Third, most harbour approaches are well lit with navigational marks which, with proper preparation and planning, should make a night arrival perfectly feasible even if it is your first time. Entering late in the day, though, may be made much more difficult if your final approach is on a westerly heading and you are squinting into the setting sun. Think twice before planning on an evening arrival near sunset!

TIP

The Solent is not unique in being plagued by poorly marked fishing gear. French fishermen usually use black flags to mark their lobster pots, but not always. For this reason I try to avoid motoring at night. If it is really necessary to do so, keep to the main shipping channels where the risk is much reduced, but maintain a very careful lookout for large ships using the same water.

Tides

It may seem that the state of the tides, springs or neaps, is largely irrelevant to a cross-Channel passage but, apart from any depth constraints on departure and arrival, the tidal streams in mid-Channel at springs run at twice the rate of neaps. Close to the French coast, or in among the Channel Islands, rates of over 5 knots at springs are the norm; in the Race of Alderney the spring flood stream reaches nearly 10 knots while at neaps this is 'only' about 4 knots. Get caught too far west off the Cotentin Peninsula on a spring ebb in a sailing yacht and you will probably wind up in Guernsey whether you like it or not. At neaps you may have a fighting chance of making ground against the stream and arriving in Cherbourg for dinner as planned.

TIP

If you leave the Solent at about high water, you will arrive (12–14 hours later) near high water on the other side if you maintain an average speed of about 5 knots. For a daytime passage across the eastern or central Channel there is another reason for choosing a period of neap tides: HW at Portsmouth or Dover will be at about 0600, which can be an ideal time to set off. In the western Channel, at Plymouth for example, times of HW are about six hours different from Dover, but as distances are significantly greater, part of the passage will almost certainly be at night anyway.

A motor yacht is not immune from the effects of tidal streams. At a speed of 15 knots and with a 5½ knot stream on the beam (the spring rate 10 miles north of Pointe de Barfleur) you will need to steer about 20° off your intended course to maintain track.

CG66

In the next chapter we look at the certificates, licences and other paperwork you will need to have before visiting France (or, indeed, most other countries). One form you should complete whatever your sailing area – inshore, coastal or offshore – is CG66, the Voluntary Safety Identification Scheme. The data you provide may prevent undue delay and help with identification should you have to call for assistance from the rescue services. In addition to your name and address, a description of the boat, safety equipment carried and your usual sailing area, the form also encourages you to give the name and contact details of someone ashore in case of emergency. There is also a facility to upload a picture of your boat.

The process is straightforward, only takes a few minutes and may be done online via the MCA website. There are no charges involved. Your form is held on the CG database for two years, after which time you will receive a reminder to update it. If you don't, it will be deleted. Paper forms are available at Maritime Rescue Coordination Centres (MRCCs), RNLI stations and many marinas and yacht clubs.

preparing for the crossing

By failing to prepare, you are preparing to fail.
Benjamin Franklin

Almost all of what follows is just as relevant to motorboats as it is to sailing yachts.

In this chapter we will first consider how to prepare the boat for the crossing, before looking at the paperwork which should be carried on board. Finally, and crucially, we need to pick our crew, with particular reference to their level of expertise and experience.

Equipment

A well fitted-out yacht which is used for coastal sailing by day and night will already have most of the gear required for a Channel crossing. A suggested list of

Safety equipment - check it all before you set off

equipment for a boat making offshore passages (50–500 miles offshore around the UK and north-west Europe) can be found at the end of this chapter, and a more comprehensive list, which takes into account the size of vessel and your intended cruising area, is in the Safety chapter in *Reeds*. Here are some of the items which need careful attention.

Liferaft

If you normally cruise in local waters in daylight, you may not own a liferaft. They are expensive to buy, but it is possible to hire one relatively cheaply for a few weeks at a time. A dinghy, with oars/paddles, towed astern or inflated and ready to launch at short notice, is an alternative but not ideal. (For years I kidded myself that a semi-inflated dinghy on the coachroof would be adequate. Once in the water it would be easy to fully inflate using the pump which had been carefully secured to one of the lifting strops. In hindsight, I am glad I never had to use it in anger: it simply would not have worked!)

Make sure a liferaft, if carried, does not become buried in a cockpit locker. It must be readily available for rapid deployment, and this is particularly important when sailing in fog. Ideally, it should be secured on deck with a hydrostatic release mechanism which allows the raft to float free if the boat sinks. If you hire one, and don't therefore have a permanent fitting for it, make sure you don't lash it down so securely that it can't be released immediately if necessary. Relying on a knife to cut through cordage is not a sensible option. Far better to use webbing with quick-release buckles.

If the worst comes to the worst, the aim is to step into the liferaft (or dinghy) without getting wet and dressed in warm waterproof clothing. However, abandoning ship is a last resort; it is invariably safer to remain with the yacht unless she is on fire or actually sinking under you.

Grab bag

Whatever means of 'escape' you have, you should also have a grab bag immediately available. The ideal bag will be waterproof and will float. The RYA recommends that the following should be included in the bag. This is by no means comprehensive and some items may already be in the liferaft; others will need to be collected at the time – so a checklist will be needed.

- Handheld VHF, fully charged and/or with spare batteries
- Handheld GPS receiver, fully charged and/or with spare batteries
- EPIRB/PLB if carried (see Chapter 9)
- Anti-seasickness tablets

- Essential medication
- Torches
- Flares
- Water

Other items might include:

- Passports
- House/car keys
- Wallet/credit cards
- Mobile phone
- Ship's papers
- Food (biscuits/snacks)

Flares

While a VHF radio is now the primary means of calling for help, if the mast falls down (and with it the VHF aerial) flares may still be your best hope of attracting attention. Suggested types and quantities are shown at the end of this chapter.

Check that all flares are in date as the French authorities take a dim view of out-of-date flares (having no flares at all is, in this context, not a problem).

Flares may attract attention at a greater range than a VHF transmission from an aerial mounted low down, such as on a motorboat's cabin top.

TIP

Relying on the use of mobile phones in a distress or emergency situation is strongly discouraged: they have limited coverage (typically no more than about 10 miles offshore); they do not 'broadcast' to other vessels which might be able to render assistance; and they are extremely vulnerable to getting wet. That said, when all other means of communications have failed, mobile phones have been used to save lives. It is not unknown for Falmouth Coastguard to be called by a vessel in distress on the other side of the world!

Fuel

Most craft (sailing and power) will have ample fuel capacity for a Channel crossing, but it is prudent to be fully topped up before setting off. Not only may a sailing yacht have to motor for 12 hours or more if the wind fails, but fuel may not be readily available at your destination, and a return trip under power may also be necessary. Calculate your engine's fuel consumption at normal cruising revolutions, and have plenty in reserve. Diesel is usually much cheaper in the Channel Islands than in the UK or France, but never rely on being able to fill up as planned. It is better to pay a bit more than run low.

Engine spares

No doubt you will already have on board at least some basic spare parts for the engine (saltwater impeller, alternator belt etc). Don't forget sufficient engine oil for a complete oil change, and a set of oil and fuel filters. Embarrassingly, many years ago, I failed to fully tighten the oil filter, which resulted in several litres of oil in my bilges – and none in the engine – necessitating a return to harbour under sail to buy some more. Furthermore, it is not uncommon to take on dirty fuel which results in blocked filters. A spare set may prevent a long search in a foreign port for the right ones.

Provisions

You are not embarking on a transatlantic passage, and there is no need to cater for three square meals a day. Indeed, a relatively inexperienced crew may be unwilling to do much cooking as they settle down into their first Channel crossing, so keep it simple. Try to have a decent meal before sailing, but nothing too rich which might cause regrets if you are susceptible to seasickness (most of us are).

For the passage, lots of tasty snacks which have been prepared ahead and are easily consumed without cutlery are ideal. Sandwiches, cakes, sweets, fruit and energy bars all go down well and, allegedly, contain no calories when sailing! In all but very rough conditions (not advised for your first crossing), it should be possible to heat up some soup and make tea or coffee. Alternatively, fill up some vacuum flasks. Hot drinks rarely go amiss, and can be a real morale booster when the going gets chilly.

TIP

You may hope to arrive in time for a good meal ashore, but remember that France is an hour ahead of the UK so local restaurants may be closing just as you finish securing the boat. As this is your first offshore passage, why not breathe a sigh of contentment and treat yourself to something special on board washed down with a good wine? Relax and enjoy – tomorrow is soon enough for sampling the culinary delights ashore.

Paperwork

You are unlikely to be asked to show any paperwork on arrival in France, but the risk of not having everything in order is not worth taking. Yachts are sometimes boarded by the French customs or marine police, at sea and in harbour, and don't expect the authorities to show much mercy if you are unable to produce the required documents. If you have all your papers to hand, preferably in a dedicated file or folder, there is nothing to worry about. Contrary to popular belief, the French customs and marine police are not out to get you; the whole process will usually be friendly and conducted professionally and efficiently. The following documents should be on board and readily available.

Certificate of Registration

Although it is not a legal requirement to register your boat if sailing in UK waters, you are very strongly recommended to do so before going abroad. Registration on Part I of the UK Ship Register enables you to prove ownership of your boat; prove your boat's nationality; use the boat as security to obtain a marine mortgage; and obtain 'Transcripts of Registry', which show the boat's previous owners and whether there are any outstanding mortgages. In 2012 the cost of registering on Part I was £124.

The cheaper, and much more usual, option is to be registered on Part III, the Small Ships Register (SSR). This is relatively inexpensive (£25 in 2012) and is equally valid in the eyes of officialdom. It shows your SSR number and boat details, including the hull identification (HID) number and the registered owner, but it is not proof of ownership. If your boat is not yet registered, you will find full details of the process at:

www.direct.gov.uk/en/TravelAndTransport/Boatingandtravellingbywater.

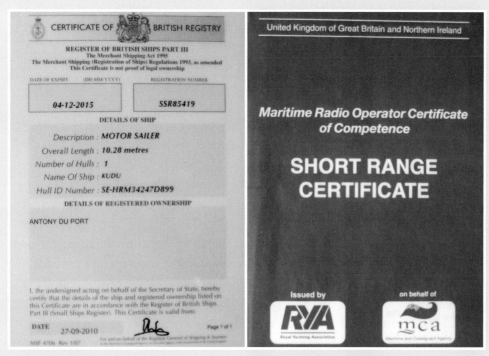

SSR certificate   **Short Range Certificate**

Proof of VAT Status

You may only use a boat within the EU if she is VAT paid or deemed to be VAT paid. VAT will normally be paid when bought from new or, if imported from outside the EU, when the vessel is imported to the UK. The rules are quite complicated, and more details can be found at *www.hmrc.gov.uk* (search for 'notice 8'). Not being able to prove that VAT has been paid could land you with a very large bill.

One exception is for boats that were in use as private pleasure craft prior to 1 January 1985, and that were in the EU on 31 December 1992. They are deemed to be VAT paid under EU single market transitional arrangements. If your boat falls into this category, you will need to be able to prove her age (builder's certificate, for example) and that she was in the EU (marina receipts, survey report etc).

Ship Radio Licence

It is a legal requirement to have a Ship Radio Licence on board and, in the wording of the licence itself, it *'shall be kept with or near to the licensed radio equipment at all times, where it is physically practicable to do so'*. All radio equipment carried on board is listed on the licence, and it will show the vessel's callsign and Maritime Mobile Service Identity (MMSI) number for DSC radios. It is an offence to use any radio equipment not covered by a Ship Radio Licence. Once obtained, it is valid for life unless surrendered by you or revoked by Ofcom (*www.ofcom.org.uk*). You also need an Authority to Operate your radio equipment (see below).

VHF Licence (Authority to Operate)

Before the radio is used, someone on board must hold an 'Authority to Operate'. This will normally be a Short Range Certificate (SRC) for VHF/DSC which is personal to the individual, and it must be carried on board. Courses are available at RYA training centres, and many clubs run their own courses on behalf of the RYA.

This does not mean that only the licence holder may operate the radio. So long as someone on board holds a licence, any crew member may operate the radio with the express permission of the licence holder, who remains responsible for all transmissions.

On inland waters your VHF radio may also need to be ATIS (Automatic Transmitter Identification System) capable, but this doesn't apply on, for example, the canal between Ouistreham and Caen. See *www.rya.org.uk* for more details.

Insurance certificate

Be sure to check that your insurer provides cover for the area you intend to visit. Most will cover you for inland and coastal waters of the UK and Ireland, and Continental waters between the Elbe and La Rochelle. Carry the original certificate, not a copy.

Recreational Craft Directive (RCD) – Declaration of Conformity

This only applies to vessels built after 16 June 1998. If for some reason you don't hold a Declaration of Conformity, you will need to contact the builder to obtain one. The penalties for not being able to produce one are severe.

If your boat was built before 16 June 1998, you should be able to provide proof, perhaps with a builder's certificate or mooring receipts, that she was in existence before that date.

> ## TIP RED DIESEL RECEIPTS
>
> Although this is not a legal requirement, many EU countries are at odds with the UK's concession which allows recreational craft to purchase red 'duty free' diesel. If you have red diesel in your tanks, keep all receipts showing where it was bought and how much duty was paid. A record of engine hours and fuel consumption will also help. Red diesel in cans is not normally permitted outside the UK and it is strongly recommended that any cans contain only white, duty paid, diesel such as you would buy from a garage ashore.

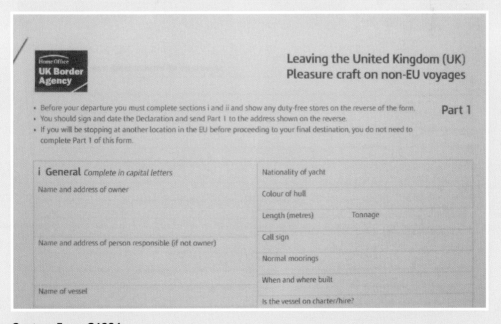

Custom Form C1331

Customs Form C1331

If you are sailing from the UK directly to the Channel Islands (which are not part of the UK or members of the EU) you must complete Form C1331 Part 1, which is available from marinas and many yacht clubs or via the HMRC website, and send it to the UK Border Agency before departure. On arrival back in the UK, Part 2 must be completed. Call the Customs National Yachtline on 0845 723 1110 for instructions. This form is not required when sailing between France, or any other EU country, and the UK, nor is it required when sailing between France and the Channel Islands.

HMRC recognises that sailing plans must be flexible, so even if you are aiming for France but wind up in the Channel Islands, you may obtain the necessary form from the harbour office or marina on arrival.

Passports

Each member of your crew must be in possession of a valid passport. Even in the Channel Islands you will need to enter passport details on the customs form on arrival. There are slight variations between the requirements of the States of Jersey and the Bailiwick of Guernsey (which comprises Guernsey, Alderney, Herm and Sark).

International Certificate of Competence (ICC)

Although not always required when sailing in coastal waters, it is strongly recommended that you carry an ICC (which may be obtained by application to the RYA) and any other proof of competence – RYA certificates, for example. If you are intending to venture inland, an ICC valid for 'inland waters' must be carried along with a copy of the CEVNI (Code Européen des Voies de la Navigation Intérieure) rules. To get this endorsement you will have to pass the CEVNI test. See *www.rya. org.uk* for details.

> TIP EUROPEAN HEALTH INSURANCE CARD (EHIC)
> Each crew member should have an EHIC. It is free, valid for five years and entitles you to reduced-cost, sometimes free, medical treatment in the EU and some other countries. Apply at *www.nhs.uk/NHSEngland/Healthcareabroad*.

The crew

So far in this chapter we have focused on preparing the boat and gathering all the relevant paperwork. We have left the most important factor until now: your crew. If this is your first Channel crossing you need to select your crew carefully. That doesn't mean that young children or other 'passengers' should not accompany you, but at least two of you must be able to sail the boat, navigate and look after the others without becoming too tired. This may be the first time you have been at sea for more than a few hours, and you will be understandably anxious to get it right. You will certainly welcome some proficient backup.

As an absolute minimum, one of you should have at least the same level of competence as an RYA Day Skipper, and one or two others, depending on the size of the boat, should be at least Competent Crew standard. In addition to yourself, at least one other crew member should be familiar with the radio and the procedures for calling for help. Consider what would happen if you became incapacitated through accident or seasickness. Would your crew have the confidence and knowledge to get the boat safely into harbour? If you have any doubts, take along a more experienced friend to support you.

Sailing and navigation are not your only concerns. You are the boss, responsible for all aspects of running the boat and her crew. Other crew members may need your help to ease the misery of seasickness, and young children may need encouragement and 'entertaining' to ward off boredom. As skipper, your prime responsibility is to keep everyone safe. If they are also happy and occupied, you are doing well. Do not underestimate how tiring this can be.

Happy crew!

TELLTALE

Children don't actually need constant attention but, if old enough, they will probably be only too willing to become involved in running the boat, looking out and steering. My two daughters have sailed offshore from the ages of 6 weeks (late starter) and 13 days respectively. They quickly learnt to amuse themselves when everyone else was too busy to pay them much attention. Excellent training for later life.

When they were very young, we used to put them, in their carrycots, in a saloon bunk with the lee cloths firmly secured. There they were perfectly safe, and we were able to keep an eye on them from the cockpit. Apart from feeding and changing, they did not affect the yacht's routine to any great extent. They slept in their carrycots and were washed in the washing up bowl. However, don't underestimate the amount of kit babies need. Every available space used to be stuffed with disposable nappies (excellent for mopping up oil in the bilges), jars of baby food and clothes, not to mention all the 'essential' toys which can't be left behind. One baby has more gear than two adults, by far.

It is later that things become rather more difficult. At the crawling/toddler stage I made dwarf bulkheads to restrain them in designated sections of the boat, and we employed old car seats, fitted with dinghy pintles, to fit in corresponding gudgeons. These worked particularly well. We had one in the cockpit, facing aft, and one either side of the main saloon. The seats had straps to keep the child secure, but we needed to remember to 'tack' the seat at the same time as the boat. If we forgot, as we did on many occasions, the child was left hanging from the straps rather like a parachutist who has got it wrong.

By the age of about 4 life becomes even more interesting. They will be fully mobile and in need of more attention. It is at about this time that two children are probably easier than one: they can make their own amusements, and a long passage works wonders, allowing their imaginations to run free. Ours occupied themselves happily for hours down below making tents out of sheets and towels, playing 'schools' with their cuddly toys and even, on one memorable Channel crossing, setting up a shop from which they 'sold' us tins of baked beans and any other goods they could find. So long as they know you are around and keeping a watch over them, they shouldn't detract from the joys of sailing. One of ours was so used to life onboard during the first 18 months of her life that she found it impossible to sleep at home without the sounds of water rushing past her bunk and the constant motion of a boat at sea.

Later still, they actually become useful crew members. Ours now both have RYA qualifications, and still sail with us when they need a free holiday.

Of course, safety is all important. We have a general rule that lifejackets are worn by everyone at night, in fog, in the dinghy and whenever we have two or more reefs in the mainsail. That said, safety harnesses are, in my view, even more vital life-savers. It should be second nature for children to wear a harness and clip on at all times – and, yes, their teddy bears as well.

Suggested safety equipment

This list is a summary of the recommended safety equipment that should be carried when crossing the English Channel or making any other passage which involves sailing more than about 50 miles offshore.

A dash (~) indicates that the number of items is left to the judgement of the skipper. It is, of course, up to you to decide exactly what equipment is appropriate, taking into account the boat and the actual passage to be undertaken.

Propulsion

■ Storm trysail or a deep reef which reduces the mainsail by at least 40% ~
■ Battery dedicated to engine starting, or the ability to start the engine by hand ~
■ Anchors, with appropriate length/size of warp and/or chain 2

Bailing and pumping

- Buckets of at least 9 litres capacity, with lanyard and strong handle **2**
- Hand bilge pumps, discharging overboard and operable with all hatches closed **2**
- Softwood bungs, attached to all through-hull fittings **~**

Detection

- Radar reflector, with as large a radar cross-section as possible **1**
- Fixed navigation lights, complying with Collision Regulations (Colregs) **~**
- Motoring cone and anchor ball **1**
- Foghorn **1**
- Powerful torches (waterproof) **~**

Flares (all in date)

- Handheld red flares **4**
- Floating orange smoke signals **2**
- Red parachute rockets **4**
- Handheld white flares ('ship scarers') **4**

Firefighting

- Fire blanket (BS EN 1869) **~**
- Multi-purpose extinguishers (minimum 5A/34B to BS EN 3) **3**
- Automatic or semi-automatic extinguisher for engine(s) (if over 25hp) **~**

Personal safety (per crew member)

- Warm clothing, oilskins, seaboots and hat **~**
- Lifejacket/buoyancy aid (BS EN 396) 150 Newtons **1**
- Crotch strap, spray hood and light for each lifejacket **1**
- Safety harness **1**
- Jackstays and cockpit strong points (for clipping on) **~**

Liferaft

- Liferaft suitable to carry all those on board **1**
- Emergency grab bag (see above for contents) **1**

Man overboard recovery

- Horseshoe lifebelts, with drogue and automatic light **2**
- Buoyant sling on floating line (may replace one lifebelt if two are carried) **1**
- Buoyant heaving line, at least 30m long, with quoit **1**

- Boarding ladder, capable of rapid attachment **1**
- Danbuoy with large flag **1**

Radio

- FM/MW/LW radio for shipping forecasts (198kHz) and local radio stations **1**
- VHF/DSC radio with emergency aerial **1**
- Waterproof handheld VHF radio **1**
- Navtex receiver **1**

Navigation

- Paper charts, tide tables, navigational publications (almanac/pilots) ~
- Navigation instruments (dividers, ruler etc) ~
- Steering compass (illuminated at night) **1**
- Hand-bearing compass ~
- Barometer **1**
- Clock or watch **1**
- Echo sounder **1**
- Radio fixing system (eg, GPS receiver) **1**
- Log (for measuring distance/speed through the water) **1**
- Binoculars **1**

First aid

- Basic first aid kit **1**

General

- Emergency tiller (for wheel-steered craft) **1**
- Warps for towing or being towed ~
- Bosun's chair **1**
- Tender (rigid or inflatable) ~
- Engine spares and tools ~
- Spare shackles, twine, etc ~
- Can(s) of fresh water (in case main tanks become contaminated) ~

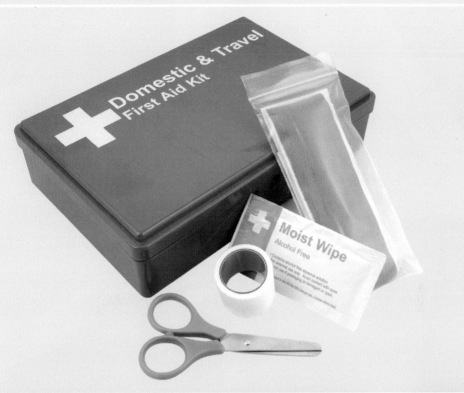

the navigational plan

A good plan is like a road map: it shows the final destination and usually the best way to get there.

H. Stanley Judd

The plan

The boat is ready, you have selected your crew, all the necessary paperwork has been checked and you have enough food on board to keep everyone fed and happy. Furthermore, the weather promises to be settled for a few days, so let's put together the navigational plan. We will look at executing the plan in Chapter 5, but for now we will consider a typical passage from the Solent to Cherbourg. The planning principles are exactly the same for any crossing of the English Channel; only the time you spend under way will vary.

It is a requirement under Chapter V of SOLAS (the International Convention for the Safety of Life at Sea) that all passages by any vessel that goes to sea must be planned. 'Going to sea' is defined as proceeding beyond sheltered waters. The Solent is considered to be 'sheltered'; the English Channel is not. At the very least, you need to determine where you are going, how to get there and what factors may influence the plan. In local waters it may be that a check of the tides and the weather forecast is all that is needed. I rarely draw any lines on my Solent charts, but I do always have them available on the chart table. However, we are planning a passage which will take us well offshore, and we need to draw up a comprehensive plan.

Good advice on passage planning (and much else) can be found in the MCA's Pleasure Craft Information Pack. Just go to *www.mcga.gov.uk* and search for the pack. *Reeds* also has comprehensive advice and a useful Passage Planning Form (see page 47) in the Navigation chapter. Perhaps rather oddly, SOLAS does not require the plan to be recorded, but in the event of any legal action arising from, say, a collision or grounding, a written plan is clear proof that the proper planning process has been completed. You can also refer to it during the passage.

The relatively severe motion, not to mention the noise, of a motorboat proceeding at speed in a choppy sea makes chartwork almost impossible. Even taking bearings using a handheld compass, or recording your position, is usually much more difficult than in a sailing yacht. For this reason, a thorough, comprehensive and workable written plan is essential. Apply the KISS principle (Keep It Safe and Simple) but be sure that all aspects are covered including pre-planned courses to steer, pilotage diagrams, transits and radar/GPS clearing bearings. A ring-bound reporter's notebook is probably ideal: it folds flat and fits inside an oilskin pocket.

When I was navigating warships around the world, I reckoned that a good pilotage plan took about twice as long to prepare as it did to execute. I am not suggesting that you necessarily need to spend a solid 24 hours planning your way from the Solent to Cherbourg, but don't underestimate the time it will take, especially for your first crossing.

TIP

Try to work undisturbed. It is remarkably easy to enter wrong numbers into a GPS waypoint list or to confuse east and west when in the vicinity of the Greenwich meridian. Once completed, however, run through the plan with someone else to check for obvious errors and give it an overall 'sanity check'. On a long north/south passage it is not impossible to miss out a whole degree of latitude, thus underestimating the overall distance by 60 miles. I know, I've done it, and my captain was not best pleased.

Cherbourg – an all-tide access port

Departure and arrival ports

You will have little choice about where to start from: it will almost invariably be your home port. However, if your normal berth is in the Hamble or the Medina you can save yourself a few hours of passage time by getting the boat to Yarmouth the day before. If leaving the Solent to the east, Gosport is a good jumping-off point.

If this is your first cross-Channel passage you are probably going to choose for your destination the nearest port which is easy to enter and where you can be sure of a secure berth, not to mention a run ashore to relax and celebrate. On the French coast, Cherbourg and St Vaast are similar distances from the Solent, but the former is free of tidal constraints and may be entered safely in any weather from any direction. Conversely, the inner approaches to St Vaast dry, the outer anchorage is uncomfortable in strong winds from the east or south, and the entry gate is open for only 2–3 hours either side of high water. Alderney is also a possibility but, as we mentioned earlier, it is impracticable in fresh winds from the north or north-east, and there are no alongside berths (although it is possible that a marina will be built in a few years' time). The strong tidal streams around the island leave little room for error, particularly if your passage is significantly faster or slower than planned. It is probably prudent to make for Cherbourg this time, leaving the delights of St Vaast or the Channel Islands for later. We will leave from Yarmouth.

Gathering the data

The Route Planner in *Reeds Digital Almanac* is useful for establishing the basics and may save you a bit of time. The notes on passage planning and the Passage Planning Form in *Reeds* (book) are good starting points when gathering your thoughts. We have covered some of this already, and now we will focus on the details.

It's wise to have a written Passage Plan with all the salient details mentioned. The Passage Planning Form (opposite, which may be copied either from this book or from *Reeds*), when completed, would constitute a reasonable passage plan as required by SOLAS Chapter V.

Charts: Dig out large-scale charts for departure and arrival, and smaller-scale charts for the offshore part of the passage. Admiralty Leisure Folios 5600 (The Solent and Approaches) and 5604 (The Channel Islands) contain most of what you need, although the latter does not include large-scale charts of Cherbourg or the coast to the east. If using these folios, you would be well advised to obtain additional charts covering Cherbourg, Pointe de Barfleur and St Vaast. Folio 5604 is perfectly adequate for the coast to the west of Cherbourg and for the Channel Islands.

DATE:........................   FROM: ....   TO:...............................   DIST: ....M

ALTERNATIVE DESTINATION(S): ....

WEATHER FORECAST: ....

FORECASTS AVAILABLE DURING PASSAGE: ....

TIDES

DATE:..............................   DATE: ....   DATE: ....

PLACE:............................   PLACE: ....   PLACE: ....

HW ....   HW ....   HW ....

LW ....   LW ....   LW ....

HW ....   HW ....   HW ....

LW ....   LW ....   LW ....

COEFFICIENT: ....

HEIGHT OF TIDE AT: ....

.... hrs   ....m   .... hrs   ....m   ....hrs   ....m

DEPTH CONSTRAINTS: ....

TIDAL STREAMS AT: ....

TURNS .... AT .... TOTAL SET (FM .... TO ....): ....° ....M

TURNS .... AT .... TOTAL SET (FM .... TO ....): ....° ....M

NET TIDAL STREAM FOR PASSAGE: ....° .... M

ESTIMATED TIME: ....hrs   ETD: ....   ETA: ....

SUN/MOON   SUNRISE: ....   SUNSET: ....

MOONRISE: ....   MOONSET: ....   PHASE: ....

WAYPOINTS   NO   NAME   TRACK/DISTANCE (TO NEXT WAYPOINT)

.... / ....

.... / ....

.... / ....

.... / ....

.... / ....

DANGERS   CLEARING BEARINGS/RANGES/DEPTHS

....

....

LIGHTS/MARKS EXPECTED ....

....

....

COMMUNICATIONS   PORT/MARINA ....   VHF ....   ☎ ....

PORT/MARINA ....   VHF ....   ☎ ....

NOTES (CHARTS PREPARED & PAGE NUMBERS OF RELEVANT PILOTS/ALMANACS/ETC): ....

....

....

TIP

Chart 5604.1 is ideal for overall planning purposes. Draw tracks in black ink from both ends of the Solent – the Needles and Nab Tower – to St Vaast, Cherbourg, Alderney and possibly Guernsey for a quick check on courses (before corrections for deviation etc) and distances. Also, highlight the shipping routes so you know when to expect busy periods.

TIP

If using a chart plotter, all the appropriate charts will be available to you. However, electronic charts cannot be corrected by the user and may be significantly out of date when you come to use them. For this trip you can do without the worry of encountering an uncharted buoy or a lighthouse with recently altered light characteristics. Also, if the electronics fail, you must have paper charts as a backup. If a chart plotter is your primary means of navigating, keep a written record in the log of your position at hourly intervals.

Tides: Look up times and heights of HW and LW for your ports of departure and arrival, and for the relevant reference ports in the tidal stream atlases and/or those shown on the tidal stream tables on the charts. The tidal stream diagram for the central English Channel in *Reeds* is referred to Dover.

You will, of course, also need to work out the predicted heights of tide for the time you expect to pass close to, or sail over, any hazards such as sandbanks which are 'tide critical' for your boat. If leaving Yarmouth at about high water and using the North Channel (see Chapter 8), for example, there would be ample depth to pass over the northern part of the Shingles Bank. At low water it would be wise to leave North Head buoy to port without cutting the corner.

TIP

A prudent navigator should always know the height of tide, approximately, at any time in order to be able to relate the actual depth (by echo sounder) to that shown on the chart. For this reason it is best to adjust your echo sounder to show the depth from the waterline. In shoal water it is a simple matter of subtracting your draught from the recorded depth to determine how much water you have under the keel. Put a note on the echo sounder display to show where the depth is measured from ('Depths from Waterline', 'Depths from Keel' etc). For example, when taking a fix you note that the depth of water by echo sounder is 22 metres. Knowing the height of tide, say 2 metres, the charted depth should be about 20 metres. If the depth on the chart is markedly different, something is wrong and you need to check your position carefully. In shallow water, if the echo sounder is showing 5 metres and your draught is 1.5 metres, you have (5 minus 1.5) 3.5 metres under the keel.

Tidal coefficients: These are shown in *Reeds* and indicate the magnitude of the tide on any particular day without having to look up and calculate the range. At a glance you can therefore determine whether it is springs, neaps or somewhere in between. The numbers to remember are:

120	Very big spring tide
95	Mean springs
70	Average tide
45	Mean neaps
20	Very small neap tide

TIP

Many French ports which are tidally constrained indicate the periods of access by a simple graph which is entered with the tidal coefficient of the day and your draught. You can see that a coefficient of, say, 40 denies access altogether. This is so much simpler than working it out from first principles.

Sunrise/sunset (also moonrise/moonset (and phase) if you are sailing at night): As already mentioned, be wary of entering a strange harbour while squinting into the setting sun. A night entry may be considerably easier (or at least less nerve-wracking) if there is a full moon and no cloud cover. Navigation lights must be shown between sunset and sunrise, and most lighthouses only show their lights between the same times.

Communications: Look up the VHF channels for the marinas or harbour authorities you may need to call, and for any relevant Vessel Traffic Services (VTS) which you may wish to monitor. In the Solent, Southampton VTS uses Ch 12. Most UK marinas monitor Ch 80, but the harbourmaster at Yarmouth is on Ch 68, and Cherbourg's Chantereyne Marina uses Ch 09. Make a note before you sail.

Chartwork

The next, very obvious, thing to do is to draw some lines on the charts. What follows applies, generally, to planning the passage on a chart plotter, but there really is no substitute for fully corrected official paper charts (eg, UKHO/Admiralty or Imray). Chart corrections can easily be downloaded from the UKHO website

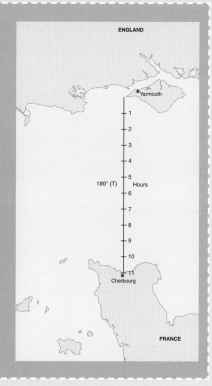

TIP

To save your precious charts, always use a soft (2B) pencil which can be rubbed out without causing too much damage. If using Leisure Folios, non-permanent pens of various colours used on the plastic cover work well. You can plot fixes and EPs (estimated positions) on two charts on the same cover, back and front. Be sure the charts are a snug fit, and always clean off the cover when you change charts. There is something disconcerting about seeing a series of neat fixes working their way across Hampshire as you change to a large-scale chart of the Solent. It helps if you can lay your hands on some spare covers – try eBay.

(Notices to Mariners) or you can use the monthly updates in *Reeds* which include all relevant notices for the area covered by the almanac.

Using the largest scale chart which ideally covers the whole passage, draw a line from the south end of the Needles Channel to the western entrance (Passe de l'Ouest) to Cherbourg outer harbour. Mark the true course (°T) and then, applying variation and deviation, work out the compass course (°C). This is not necessarily the course to steer (see below).

TIP

You may find it easier to do all your navigational work in °C, but be consistent. It doesn't really matter so long as everyone knows what '193°' means: True, Magnetic or Compass.

In practice, it is less confusing and quicker to measure the magnetic bearing from the compass rose and allow for any deviation on that heading, subtracting easterly deviation and adding westerly to get the compass course (°C). Check the notation on the compass rose to make sure the magnetic offset is up to date. If not, make the necessary adjustment. Variation in the English Channel in 2012 was less than 2.5°W and decreasing but should not be ignored as any deviation in the same direction will combine to make a significant compass error.

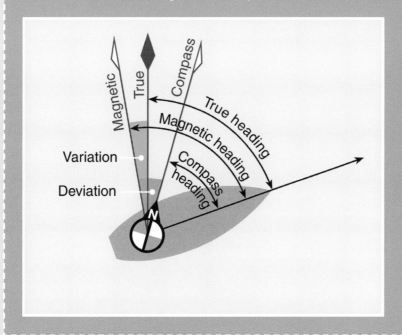

Next, measure the distance using the latitude scale on the side of the chart (you know that, but some people still get it wrong!), and calculate the approximate crossing time using your best guess for boat speed in the prevailing conditions. If anything, underestimate your speed and overestimate the time – it does wonders for morale if you arrive earlier than planned. On this passage the tidal streams will not make much difference to the total passage time as we will be sailing at roughly 90° to the direction of flow. If your track was more slanted into, or with, the tidal stream, you would of course need to take it into account. We will look at the course to steer to allow for tidal streams in a moment, but you now have all the information you need to decide on your estimated times of departure (ETD) and arrival (ETA).

TIP

Fighting a spring flood stream in the Hurst Narrows and Needles Channel is not a good idea, so aim to leave Yarmouth while the stream is on the ebb: one hour before to four hours after HW Portsmouth. HW Portsmouth at neaps is at about 0600, so you could leave Yarmouth between 0500 and 1000 - ideal for an ETA in Cherbourg between about 1700 and 2200. The earlier you can persuade your crew to get going within this time window, the more chance of a daylight entry and a run ashore on arrival. This is not quite so easy to achieve at springs but is still possible with a very early start. The alternative would be to leave during the late afternoon and arrive before breakfast. But, as we said in Chapter 2, you may prefer to make your first crossing during the hours of daylight.

TELLTALE

Whenever we meet, the erstwhile commanding officer of a minesweeper to which I was temporarily appointed as navigator reminds me of an embarrassing time when I missed out an entire degree of latitude in my passage plan from Plymouth to the Clyde.

From Land's End our track took us due north to a position west of St David's Head, a distance of about 120 miles, or 2° of latitude. Now, when you are in a hurry and feeling seasick it is surprisingly simple to miss out a chart altogether. In this case it was the one between 50°30'N and 51°30'N.

I had carefully plotted the track transferring positions from one chart to the other using longitude 6°W (as far as I remember) but misreading the latitude. In an old Ton class wooden minesweeper, 60 miles takes a good 5 hours at passage speed. We made up some of that time, but I am still haunted by the thought of HMS ... arriving in the Clyde several hours later than planned.

Lesson learnt: check and double check when drawing up the track, and be sure to transfer your position from chart to chart by latitude & longitude and by a range & bearing from a charted object.

Tidal streams

Now open the tidal stream atlas and mark it up with the times of high water. If using the Admiralty Tidal Stream Atlas NP 250, the times are referred to HW at Dover; in *Reeds* times are shown for Dover, Cherbourg and Brest. From this, for each hour add up the distance the stream will set you to the east and to the west. Subtract the lower figure from the higher to establish the overall set. As an example the figures might be:

Hours from Needles	Tidal set west	Tidal set east	Overall set
1	2.2W		2.2W
2	3.0W		5.2W
3	1.5W		6.7W
4	Slack	Slack	6.7W
5		2.0E	4.7W
6		4.0E	0.7W
7		4.2E	3.5E
8		4.0E	7.5E
9		0.5E	8.0E
10	1.0W	7.0E	
11	1.0W	6.0E	
Total	8.7W	14.7E	6.0E

So, 6 miles to the east is the figure you need in order to calculate your course to steer. This is not a precise science as it depends on your actual progress. If you make better speed than planned, you will be in the much stronger streams off the Cotentin Peninsula earlier than planned. Similarly, a slower passage may mean the stream has already turned by the time you get there. You will need to monitor this as you go, making suitable course adjustments as necessary. In the 'old days' when navigation tended to be less precise (no GPS or radar), it was good practice to aim to arrive several miles upstream, and ideally upwind, of your destination. By doing so, not only did you then have a downstream passage to make port, you also had a good idea of which way to turn when you sighted land. Don't be fooled into thinking that a 12-hour passage means that the streams will cancel out. The harder streams near the French coast will soon prove you wrong, and if you don't do your sums you will wish you had.

Course to steer

The next step is to work out your course to steer using a simple vector diagram. In the situation described above, which assumes a boat speed of 5½ knots, the track on the chart is 180° but the course to steer will be nearer 185°.

The Needles: a popular 'jumping off' point from the Solent

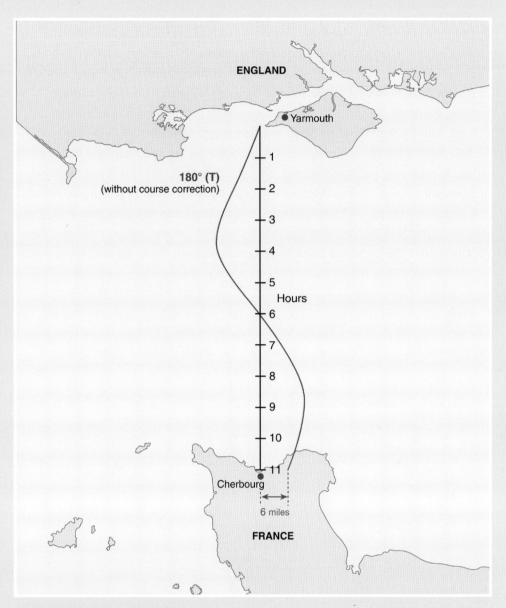

ENGLAND

● Yarmouth

180° (T)
(without course correction)

1
2
3
4
5
Hours
6
7
8
9
10
11
Cherbourg

6 miles

FRANCE

Track with no course correction

TIP

Always try to select courses to steer ending in a '0' or '5'. The helmsman will find it much easier, and will therefore probably helm more accurately, if he/she is asked to steer 185° rather than 183° or 187°. Mark this on the chart in parentheses after the compass course (°C).

By the time you are approaching Cherbourg (ten hours from the Needles) the stream will be setting to the west and will continue to do so for another 4–5 hours. You need, therefore, to monitor your course over the ground (COG) very carefully to ensure you are not set to the west of Passe de l'Ouest. If you have planned to enter via Passe de l'Est, you can allow yourself to be swept down to Passe de l'Ouest, but this would not be good navigational practice!

You may be tempted to maintain the track on the chart throughout the passage, adjusting your course each hour in order to do so. This is not the most efficient way of conducting the passage and you will be sailing for longer. Allow the stream to set you off track while you sail on the same heading. Not only does this mean that you will sail less distance through the water, but you will also be able to admire the S-shaped track on the chart that you describe over the ground.

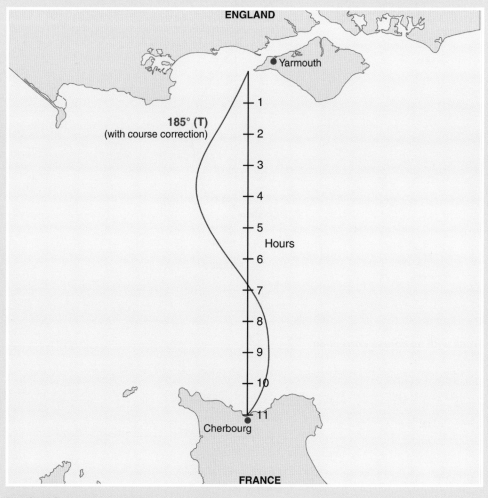

Track with course correction

Clearly, you must make sure that you have the room, navigationally, to allow the boat to be set this far off the planned track. In this passage, there is no problem, but bear this in mind if you are sailing in restricted waters.

This is not as critical for a motorboat travelling at 20 knots as the extra distance, and therefore time, involved in maintaining the track will be minimal. However, the principle still applies, and you may save a few drops of fuel!

Plot the track

Finally, transfer your track onto larger-scale charts so you are always navigating on the largest scale practicable. If you are planning to be sailing at night (or if you might still be out after sunset due to delays), mark on the charts the ranges where you expect to see shore lights. Look up a lighthouse's elevation and, entering Table 3(6) in *Reeds* with your own height of eye, read off the range when it will rise above the horizon if the prevailing visibility allows.

Although not particularly relevant to a Channel crossing between the Needles and Cherbourg, you should also note any dangers en route (shallow water, rocks, buoys, lights etc) and mark them clearly on the chart with a thick black pencil. For this passage, mark the main shipping routes by drawing lines in ink connecting the western end of the Dover Strait traffic separation scheme (TSS) with the eastern end of the Casquets TSS. You will then be able to estimate when you are likely to be in the thick of the commercial traffic as it ploughs up and down the Channel.

Alternative destinations

You are now, navigationally, nearly ready to go. Before casting off, consider what you will do if the weather turns nasty, if you suffer gear failure or if one of the crew becomes ill or has an accident, any of which could necessitate a change of plan. The variables are too numerous to list, but you need to plan bolt-holes on the English south coast should you decide to turn back after a few hours. On this passage a return to the Solent via the Needles Channel may be a good bet, but wind and weather may mean that Weymouth, Poole or the eastern entrance to

the Solent would be more prudent. Remember that the Needles Channel is best avoided if the wind is strong from the south or south-west, particularly against the ebb tide.

On the French side there are not too many options, but shelter from the west may be found east of Barfleur (with St Vaast a few miles further south). To the west, the only possible option without committing yourself to the Race of Alderney is Alderney itself. However, as we have already said, Cherbourg poses no navigational problems and can be entered safely even in a strong northerly wind, by day or night. Should you enter at speed and in some disarray, as I have on several occasions, there is plenty of room in the outer harbour to get things under control before making a sedate approach to the Petite Rade and the marina.

TIP

Having completed this stage of the planning process, you might think it is a good time to indulge in some light reading and brush up on the Colregs. You will meet large commercial vessels in the shipping lanes, and there is always the possibility of fog or poor visibility. More on this later.

Opposite top: *Sailing in blustery conditions*
Opposite bottom: *Pointe de Barfleur*

setting off

If one does not know to which port one is sailing, no wind is favourable.
Lucius Seneca

Weather

In Chapter 2 we discussed the advisability of checking the weather forecasts so that you build up a picture of the developing weather pattern. The Met Office provides an excellent surface pressure forecast which will indicate any predicted changes to the weather for the next 84 hours. If it looks as though it is becoming unsettled, consider delaying your passage until you can be reasonably sure of favourable conditions, not only for the initial crossing but also for the return trip. After all, this is your first Channel crossing and you will have enough to think about without the added worry of uncertain weather.

TIP

There is absolutely no shame in deciding to delay or even abandon your trip because the weather is not right. At the time you may feel a bit of a wimp as others set off into a southerly force 5, but your crew will bless your good judgement when the same boats return to harbour having given up after a few miles.

Listen to the early morning shipping forecast at 0520 on BBC Radio 4 (FM, MW and LW) which includes reports from coastal stations and the inshore forecast. Alternatively, nip up to the harbour office and see if the latest forecast has been posted. Failing that, listen to the Maritime Safety Information (MSI) broadcast from Solent Coastguard on VHF Channel 23 or 86 after an initial announcement on Ch 16. This includes the shipping and inshore forecasts and is broadcast at 0730, so you might already be under way. Listen to it anyway just in case something unexpected has cropped up which causes you to think again.

Shore contact

Tell someone ashore of your plans and what they should do if you don't contact them on arrival. You should also give them the contact details of the coastguard station (MRCC) which holds your CG66. The onus is on you as the coastguard will not take any action unless they are alerted by you or your contact ashore.

TIP

With a good VHF aerial at the top of a yacht's mast it is usually possible to raise Solent Coastguard all the way to Cherbourg, and there is no harm in reporting your safe arrival. But don't forget to tell your shore contact as well, by phone, email or text message.

Having a much lower aerial, a motorboat should be able to talk with a shore station, such as Solent Coastguard, until about halfway across the Channel. Contact with Solent Coastguard from Cherbourg would defy the laws of physics.

Briefing the crew

Crew briefing

Brief your crew. By now you will have a clear plan in your head and on paper, but your crew will appreciate being put fully in the picture. This is also a good opportunity to check your safety equipment: danbuoy, lifejackets, safety harnesses, jackstays etc. Most of what follows can easily be done the evening before sailing:

TELLTALE

A good example of poor crew briefing involved a girlfriend who was relatively new to yachting. We had to move the boat from a temporary berth within our small marina to our permanent berth, where the mooring lines were already secured to the pontoon. The plan was for me to motor round to the new berth while my girlfriend waited to throw me the lines as I came alongside. What could go wrong? As I approached, with a stiff breeze blowing me off, I called (she later claimed I shouted) for her to throw me the rope by her left foot. Nothing happened. Slowing down, I called/shouted louder for the same rope. Eventually, it was a full bellowed roar as I rapidly made leeway, and the opportunity for a neat berthing alongside was ruined.

Her defence during the subsequent 'post mortem' was that the rope I wanted was by her right foot! I learnt two things: sort out your left and right, and don't shout. A thorough briefing beforehand would have solved the problem. We have now been married for more than 20 years.

Navigational plan

Spread out the chart and show them the planned track, where they can expect to enter shipping lanes, any prominent features to look out for as you approach the French coast (eg, the chimneys of the nuclear plant at Cap de la Hague and the lighthouse at Pointe de Barfleur) and, if relevant, where you expect to be at sunrise/sunset.

Personal preparations

It used to be said that you should wear as much as you think you will need, and then put on one more layer. Modern sailing clothing is warmer and lighter than in days past, but the principle still stands. It is a great deal easier to strip off a layer or two as the day warms up than to go below and put on more clothes when you have already started getting cold. While woolly hats are a bonus, gloves need some thought. Wet woolly gloves are miserable, and they can become snagged in ropes and winches. The best are those designed for sailing which allow your fingers to stick out of the ends. I once sailed with a Royal Marines officer who insisted on wearing a tie at all times. This was stretching sartorial elegance to a ridiculous degree, but it gave us much amusement as we longed for the tie to become inextricably entwined around the jib winch. Sadly, it never did.

Even if your crew claim to be immune to seasickness, you should encourage them to take precautions. If taking pills, follow the instructions which normally advise the first dose several hours before sailing. I very rarely become ill at sea, but I always take a pill before the first Channel crossing of the season or if it is likely to be a bit lumpy. As skipper you can't afford to take the risk of being laid low.

Slap on the suncream. Sunburn is far more likely at sea, with noses, lips and ears being especially vulnerable, even when the sun isn't shining.

Watchkeeping

For this daytime passage, you may not bother to keep formal watches. Most of us can stay awake and alert for 18 hours or so, but short watches of even one or two hours can help to settle the crew into a routine and provide recognised periods of rest – particularly if it is a bit rough. If you are sailing at night, when your natural body cycle tells you that you should be tucked up in bed, follow a routine which allows (indeed, encourages) periods of undisturbed rest. If possible, avoid keeping a watch yourself. Rest when you can, and be available when you are needed. Drum into your team that you will never mind being roused if they think it is necessary, however grumpy you may sound and feel at the time.

Safety

The unusual motion of the open sea may catch some of your crew unawares. Stress the 'one hand for you, one for the boat' rule. In other words, hold on firmly when moving about the deck. Establish your policy for wearing lifejackets and harnesses, and be sure everyone knows how they work. Many people now wear a lifejacket at all times when under way, and that is certainly what the RNLI recommends. They should always be worn at night, in rough weather (if it's windy enough for a couple of reefs in the mainsail, it is probably rough enough to put on lifejackets) and in fog.

These rules apply equally to harnesses: it is a good idea to wear them at the same time as lifejackets. Brief the crew about fitting them correctly, and where they should be clipped on. You should have strong points in the cockpit, and jackstays along the decks. Avoid running rigging and guard wires. The overriding priority is to stay on board as recovering a man overboard (MOB) is far, far more difficult than it may seem from exercises with a fender, and probably impossible if you are short-handed, unless you are very lucky.

In rough weather, it is good practice to clip on, if possible, before emerging fully into the cockpit. Similarly, don't unclip until you are safely below again.

MOB

You will be very unlucky if someone actually falls over the side. Indeed, if everyone obeys the rules – holding on, wearing harnesses – there really is no excuse, but it can happen and all crew members must be thoroughly briefed on the MOB routine. They must also be familiar with the equipment: lifebelts, danbuoys etc. The aim is to get the casualty back on board as quickly as possible taking into account sea conditions, wind/weather, experience of the crew and the manoeuvrability of the boat.

As skipper, it is for you to decide if you are going to take the helm yourself or stand back and direct the MOB recovery. This will depend on your confidence in the helmsman at the time; manoeuvring the boat is only one of several things which you must oversee. The following actions are in rough order of priority but should all happen almost simultaneously:

Shout 'Man Overboard!' It doesn't matter if everyone has seen the person fall over the side, shout anyway. It will galvanise your crew and, properly briefed, they should start taking the necessary actions without being told.

Get a crew member to look and point at the MOB Make absolutely certain that the crew member who is detailed to look and point at the MOB does nothing else and is not distracted by what is going on around him/her. Once lost from view, it might be very hard to find the casualty again.

Throw a lifebuoy and/or danbuoy over the side The more life-saving gear you get into the water, the better. At night be sure that at least one of the lifebuoys/danbuoys has a light attached to it. It may seem counter-intuitive but a fixed light is more easily seen than a flashing strobe light, especially in choppy seas.

Manoeuvre the boat to get into a suitable position If you have a spinnaker set, get it down fast. Once hove-to (see below), consider lowering all sails and making the final approach to the MOB under power, having checked for stray lines in the water which could foul the prop. Ideally you need to be stopped upwind and close to the casualty.

TIP

There is plenty of advice about manoeuvring to recover an MOB. In the heat of the moment you need a plan which is simple and foolproof (the KISS principle again). Years of experience – never 'for real', thank goodness – have convinced me that heaving-to immediately is the best option. Simply put the boat through the wind as quickly as possible without tacking the foresail. Most boats will settle down more or less beam to the wind and be almost stopped in the water. Crucially, you will still be close to the MOB and in a good position to lower sails and start the engine. There must be nothing more dispiriting to a person in the water than to see the yacht sailing away on a beam reach to complete some easily forgettable manoeuvre.

Press the MOB key on the GPS/chart plotter This is particularly relevant at night and will give you a geographical aiming point should you lose sight of the casualty. However, both the boat and the MOB will be affected by the tidal stream, and you must take this into account.

Make preparations for recovery Each boat is different. In calm seas, and if the casualty is able to help him/herself, it might be possible to recover the MOB via a bathing ladder on the stern. However, a midships recovery position is usually safer. Do you have a ladder which can be quickly rigged? Can you release the guardrails to make life easier? If the MOB is weak or unconscious it will be extremely difficult to get him/her back onboard; do you have a plan for rigging a block and tackle to hoist the casualty onboard? Forethought and preparation are the keys to a successful outcome.

Distress call In general terms, a MAYDAY (Distress) call is fully justified for a MOB situation. Whether you actually do this, by DSC or voice, will depend on the circumstances. In calm seas and benign conditions when the MOB is likely to be quickly recovered, a Distress call is possibly unnecessary. If in doubt and recovery is going to be difficult or you are having problems finding the casualty, make the appropriate call. As skipper you are required on deck so have a suitably briefed crew member operating the radio.

Emergency procedures

This will be covered in more detail in Chapter 9. It may be you who is disabled, so at least one other member of the crew must be able to operate the radio and know how to make an Urgency or Distress call, by DSC and by voice.

Call the Coastguard

Just before casting off you need to give the Coastguard a call with your passage plan (directly on Ch 67 for Solent Coastguard; Ch 16 elsewhere). Have a prepared checklist to ensure nothing is missed: name of vessel, callsign, MMSI number, port of departure (and time), destination and ETA, number of people on board and which MRCC holds your CG66.

You are ready to go!

the crossing

It is not the ship so much as the skilful sailing that assures the prosperous voyage.
George William Curtis

Departure

The crossing starts from the moment you get under way, but for this passage we will assume you have safely left Yarmouth, negotiated the Hurst Narrows and are now at the south-west end of the Needles Channel, with the lighthouse abeam. This is the time to mark your position on the chart and note your 'departure' in the log. This may seem pedantic, but it is the starting point of the crossing from where all subsequent calculations of position will be based.

Yes, you probably have a GPS and a chart plotter, but a good navigator will always check the boat's position by all means possible. Paper charts and the log do not rely on a power source, and they will withstand knocks and salt water while remaining perfectly useable.

A good sailing breeze off the Needles

EP

Your departure fix may be noted as a latitude and longitude, a range and bearing from an object or just 'close abeam Bridge Buoy'. It does not really matter so long as, *in extremis*, someone else can establish exactly where you are at any given time. From there, steer the course you have already calculated and plot an estimated position (EP) for at least an hour ahead. The distance run in the next hour will, of course, depend on your speed through the water and the effects of the tidal stream. Mark the EP, with a time, on the chart.

If your next fix is not close to the EP something is wrong. Don't assume it is your calculations: it may be that the GPS is playing up (unlikely but possible) or that you have plotted one or both positions incorrectly. Again, try to obtain your position using as many sources as possible: GPS, visual bearings, radar ranges and depth.

> ## TIP
>
> Remember the value of the echo sounder. Allowing for the height of tide, compare the recorded depth with that shown on the chart. If it is wildly different, you may not be where you think you are.

What course?

If you can't steer the planned course because of the wind direction, you will need to decide which tack to be on. Normally, this will be the one which is closest to the track. You then have the option of beating between 'tramlines' drawn, say, three miles either side of the track, or accepting a large cross-track error for a time.

Discussions abound on whether it is better to choose the tack which puts the stream on the lee bow or to 'go with the flow'. Many factors, notably the predicted changes in the tidal set and forecast wind shifts, will help you to decide how to make best progress towards your destination. It may be that the wind is kicking up a lumpy sea which may calm down when the stream changes. If so, comfort may take precedence over speed.

Whatever you do, always keep firmly in mind the aim of the passage: to arrive safely with a happy crew. To this end, you may need to spend some time at the chart table to formulate your tactics to give you a fighting chance of getting you to a position uptide of your destination in a reasonable time.

Once you have settled down into 'passage routine', enjoy the sailing! As a rule of thumb, update your EP every hour and then plot a fix on the chart.

> ## TIP
>
> The mid-Channel shipping lanes provide remarkably accurate 'lines of position'. Each one is only about 5 miles wide with a 5 mile gap between them. Most ships follow them closely, so you should be able to estimate your north/south position to within a couple of miles as you cross them.

TELLTALE

We were sailing from St Malo to the Solent in the same 'windfall' yacht mentioned in a previous Telltale. It was night, the visibility was poor and we were tired after a good run ashore in France. I have forgotten the details of the navigational plan, but I came on deck in the early morning to see Alderney – as reported by the watch leader – slipping past some miles to the south east. Something didn't quite compute: if that was Alderney, where were the Casquets, and what was the lighthouse doing in the sea instead of on the north east tip of the island?

This time, the plan was sound but the equipment let us down. Remember, this was long before the days of GPS, radar and chart plotters. It turned out that the steering compass, which was mounted on a board between the cockpit sides, had been knocked during the night causing it to flip over so that north became south. Subsequent tests also showed that it was quite possible for the compass card to stick when heeled more than a few degrees – especially if it was reading back to front. The resulting 'errors' (no more than about 180°!) had led the watch on deck to believe we were off the north-west coast of Alderney, not Guernsey as proved to be the case.

I suspect that most of us would 'feel' that something was wrong in a similar situation, and anyhow regular fixing by GPS or radar would save the day. The obvious lesson is: don't rely on just a couple of sources of information (in our case an inaccurate compass and a dodgy log). Fix by all means available, bearing in mind that the echo sounder can often give the first hint that something is wrong.

Back to basics

Should the electronics fail, you must have confidence in your plotted position, within a mile or so, at any time. If you are unable to get a fix for a few hours you need to factor in all the possible errors in your course and speed over the ground, COG and SOG respectively. You may assume a 5% error in the log readings, both in speed and distance run. Similarly, no helmsman is capable of steering an absolutely accurate course. The tabulated tidal stream at any position and time is only a prediction and should not be relied on. If you pass close to a moored fishing float or navigational buoy, see how the stream is running in reality.

TIP

Make a habit of asking the helmsman what course has *actually* been steered, on average, during the last hour. Emphasise that an honest answer is much more valuable than an answer he or she thinks you want to hear. Allow for an error of, say, 3° either side anyway. A good tip is to change helmsmen at the same time as you plot your EP, probably every hour on the hour. You will then have only one 'error' to worry about. If an autopilot is engaged, don't assume it is following the course set. It will probably be more consistent than its human counterpart but make sure someone is monitoring the course it is actually steering. The rougher the sea, the more inaccuracy you can expect – by man or machine.

A new crew member on the helm

Finally, consider leeway, which can only be estimated and may be at least 5° when beating into a stiff breeze and a lumpy sea; it will be close to zero when running downwind. Taking all these factors into consideration, you will arrive at an overall error in course over the ground (COG) and speed over the ground (SOG). This may typically be ±5° in heading and ±5% in distance run.

Pool of errors

You are now able to plot a cone of courses 5° either side of your best estimate, and about 0.25 miles ahead and astern of your estimated distance. This gives you a 'pool of errors', or 'circle of probability' (in fact, an oddly shaped box), around your EP. Assume your position is on that part of the box which is closest to danger. In this case, the 'danger' will be the nearest land ahead. The circle will keep expanding until you are able to get a good fix, when it will, of course, reduce to nothing. If you are really unlucky, the circle will become so large that it touches a real hazard. At this point, especially in poor visibility, you must accept that you are putting the boat and your crew at risk. The only safe course of action is to steer away from the hazard until you can positively establish your position.

As we have said before, but it is worth repeating, the motion of a powerboat at speed makes it well-nigh impossible to use the chart table, so a concise passage plan is essential; make a note of all waypoints, courses to steer etc in the log. A relatively high speed and short passage time does much to negate the effects of tidal streams but, if the GPS/chart plotter should fail, your only option may be to slow down sufficiently to enable you to carry out some old-fashioned chartwork.

Shipping lanes

Although mandatory when crossing a TSS, it is only 'recommended' that you cross the Channel shipping lanes at 90° to the general flow of traffic. On this passage your track will be about 180°, while vessels in the shipping lanes are steering approximately 255°/075°. So you will need to steer about 165° to comply. While 15° may not seem much, if you don't do this and you are already steering 20° 'uptide' to maintain your track in a strong flood tidal stream, your heading will be nowhere near the required 90°.

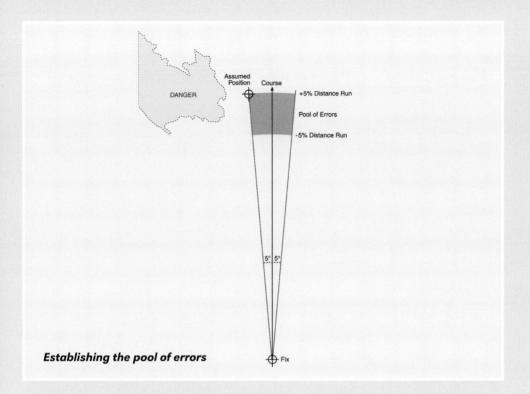

Establishing the pool of errors

It is your *heading* which counts, not the track over the ground. A dog-leg to obey the recommendation will add a few miles to the overall distance but at least you will be legally in the clear. If the wind doesn't allow you to sail close to this heading, consider motoring or motorsailing for the 5 miles to get across each lane.

Collision avoidance

You should already have a good working knowledge of the International Regulations for Preventing Collisions at Sea (IRPCS) – usually shortened to just 'Collision Regulations' or 'Colregs' – and will probably be used to dodging other vessels in your local waters. A cross-Channel passage poses a few extra challenges. First, although much of the commercial shipping follows the recommended routes between the Strait of Dover and the Off Casquets TSS, they are big and travelling fast: 25 knots is not uncommon.

Secondly, depending on which part of the Channel you are sailing in, you will be in amongst the cross-Channel ferries plying from Weymouth, Poole and Portsmouth to St Malo, the Channel Islands, Cherbourg and Le Havre. Many of these will be steaming at up to 27 knots, while the high-speed ferries are capable of speeds in excess of 40 knots. They have schedules to meet, and don't slow down if they can possibly avoid doing so.

Thirdly, many ships necessarily navigate outside the recommended routes on their way to Portsmouth, Southampton, Cherbourg and Le Havre. Add to this fishing vessels and other yachts and you will appreciate that the Channel can be a busy place.

TIP

Your fundamental problem is to decide which vessels pose a risk of collision or a close-quarters situation. Don't ignore the others in case of unexpected alterations of course, but they are of relatively low priority. You can establish whether a ship's relative bearing is changing significantly by steering a steady course, sitting still and observing it over the guardrail stanchions. But I don't think this is nearly as accurate as taking bearings with a handheld compass. The best hand-bearing compasses are those with a stout rubber surround, a lit scale and a cord to hang round your neck. Most are remarkably sturdy and accurate. The actual *bearing* is irrelevant; it is the change of bearings that should concern you. Remember that the bows of a large container ship may be drawing clear, but what about the stern?

There is no hard and fast rule which defines 'clear' or 'danger'; it's a matter of judgement depending on many factors including weather, visibility, manoeuvrability and other shipping in the immediate area. In good visibility, I would be very wary of crossing ahead of a large ship with a Closest Position of Approach (CPA) of less than a mile. In rough weather or poor visibility, I would at least double that. Far better to pass astern if you can do so safely and within the spirit of the Colregs.

Interpretation of the Colregs

One school of thought is to keep well clear of all big ships at all times. Others advocate obeying the Colregs to the letter: if you are the stand-on vessel, maintain your course and speed regardless of the fact that you are a 5-ton yacht making 6 knots and the opposition is a 100,000-ton container ship doing 25 knots. Both views have their merits, but neither meets the spirit of the rules. A bit more thought is required.

A yacht is very, very difficult to see from the bridge of a large ship. This is made worse if there are many white horses (force 5 or above) as a white yacht with white sails will blend nicely into the background, and you are not going to show up well on radar, if at all. Although the rules are quite clear about keeping a good lookout, it seems that many large-ship watchkeepers are now relying more and more on radar and AIS for collision avoidance rather than their eyes and binoculars. Never assume that you have been seen.

You will encounter the west-bound shipping about 20 miles south of the Needles, or about four hours into the passage. Whether sailing or motoring, you are the stand-on vessel, but how far are you going to push it?

The best advice may be to invoke Rule 17(a)(ii) nice and early. This rule allows the stand-on vessel to '... *take action to avoid collision by her manoeuvre alone, as soon as it becomes apparent to her that the vessel required to keep out of the way is not taking appropriate action...*'. This means that you don't have to stand on with gritted teeth hoping that the other vessel is going to alter course for you before it is too late. You are perfectly within your rights to make a bold alteration of course or speed to avoid a close-quarters situation. But make sure it is early and obvious. Slowing down from 6 knots won't make any significant difference and is unlikely to be apparent to another vessel. A large alteration of course is almost always preferable.

TELLTALE

In most cases it is clear who is the stand-on vessel and who should give way, but not always. While in command of an offshore patrol vessel, I was enjoying a film one night in the wardroom as we made passage from Plymouth to Portsmouth. The Officer of the Watch (OOW) called me to say there was a medium-sized coaster on our port bow at a range of about four miles; she was on a steady bearing. The OOW intended to maintain course and speed, and I agreed. It was a clear, dark night with a calm sea and little wind, but I had my doubts. As I arrived on the bridge, I saw the ship 10° on the port bow, still on a steady bearing. We were about 10° on her starboard bow. As there was plenty of sea room all around, there was no reason why the coaster should not abide by Rule 14 and alter her course to starboard to pass 'red to red'. By this time the range had closed to two miles and mental alarm bells were ringing. I was loath to alter course to starboard as we would then be crossing her bows; an alteration to port or a reduction in speed were clearly out of the question as we would be setting ourselves up for a collision if the other vessel decided, at the last moment, to obey the Colregs.

We tried calling her on VHF, and we shone a light on her bows, but to no effect. In the end, at a range of less than a mile, I made a hard turn to starboard using full rudder and plenty of power. The coaster passed about two cables under our stern as we continued our 360° turn to resume our track. As she passed we were able to read her name and port of registry, and we called her again on VHF. We also shone a more powerful light on the bridge area but saw no sign of life. The incident was reported to Solent Coastguard, but I never received any feedback.

Should we have invoked Rule 17? I don't think so, as an alteration of course to starboard, the only viable option, would have taken us across the coaster's bows at an uncomfortably close range. Anyhow, why should we? The situation was perfectly clear, and there was no reason, initially, to suppose the other vessel would not do the decent thing. The fact that we couldn't raise her on VHF or see anyone on board was a concern, but the lesson learnt was that even a relatively simple situation can turn nasty very quickly. I have no doubt that a collision would have resulted if we had stood on for any longer.

Breathing a sigh of relief, I returned below to catch the last reel of the film.

If you are doing 20 knots in a motor yacht, slowing down to 5 knots will clearly make a difference. But any alteration of speed *on its own* is unlikely to fully satisfy the spirit of the Colregs because it is never immediately obvious to the other ship – unlike a bold alteration of course, which is.

The east-bound shipping, about 35 miles south of the Needles, will be approaching on your starboard bow and, if you are motoring, you will be the give-way vessel. If sailing, you are, as above, the stand-on vessel, but invoking Rule 17(a)(ii) is a relatively safe option and will put ships on your port bow and enable you to pass 'red to red'. Do this early enough and life becomes much simpler.

If you are the give-way vessel, you are bound to monitor the situation and keep well clear until any risk of collision has passed.

Domestic issues

Let us turn our thoughts to domestic issues. Are your crew getting cold, hungry, thirsty or bored? In all cases, the solutions are pretty obvious. Most of us tend to

Fast passage in the Solent

graze our way across the Channel. There is no reason to abandon mealtimes if you don't want to, but a steady supply of sandwiches, soup, chocolate and other goodies does wonders for the spirits – ask any child. Some skippers run a 'dry' ship and forbid any alcohol consumption while under way. If you do not subscribe to that, moderation is vital. Everyone on board is, directly or indirectly, responsible for some aspect of safety, if only for maintaining a lookout. A good rule of thumb is to limit alcohol consumption to keep below the drink-drive limit (which is actually the law, but generally accepted to be unenforceable). If you are involved in any 'incident', there is a good chance you could be breathalysed.

Tackling boredom

Boredom can be a bit of a problem as there is a limit to the number of crew required just to keep the boat 'straight and level'. An established rota for helming, looking out and providing sustenance will help to keep the crew occupied.

TIP

There is no reason for you to do all the navigation. Delegate to others and watch the satisfaction they get from plotting a fix or working up an EP. Personally, when things are quiet, I never pass up the opportunity for a nap.

Night sailing

At night you cannot see the ships themselves and their ranges are harder to determine, but changing aspects of their, and your, lights makes any alterations of course much more obvious. If you have radar, Rule 5 implies that you should use it in order to maintain a good lookout (*by all available means*), and 7(b) says that *proper use shall be made of radar equipment if fitted*. Limited battery capacity may make this impracticable, but you should at least have the radar on standby (which uses almost no power) so that you can obtain the range of another ship at short notice. In poor visibility you would be most unwise not to have the radar transmitting, motoring if necessary to keep the batteries charged.

TIP

As a note of caution, 'radar-assisted collisions' are not uncommon. Get some tuition in its proper use, and become familiar with your particular equipment by practising in clear visibility.

While we are thinking of sailing at night, let us look briefly at some of the additional preparations and precautions you need to take. If you have not done much before, you might be a bit apprehensive, but night sailing can be fun. If you haven't been in the cockpit at first light as the smell of bacon wafts up from the galley, you haven't lived! As always, preparation is the key.

■ Make sure all the crew wear **harnesses** and **lifejackets** (fitted with properly adjusted crotch straps) whenever they come up from below. With everyone clipped on, the cockpit can end up with a bit of a snakes' wedding of safety lines, but don't be tempted to relax this rule as you will be very lucky to find and recover a man overboard in the dark. For that reason, anyone going on deck must clip on, preferably to a suitable jackstay, before leaving the cockpit.

■ Show the appropriate **navigation lights**, but keep others to a minimum. A cigarette lighter, a bright cabin light or a chart plotter's illumination turned up too high can impair your night vision for up to 20 minutes.

■ Have a torch to hand which is powerful enough to light up the sails if you are in any doubt about whether another vessel has seen you.

■ Have a white 'ship scarer' **flare** available.

■ Choose a **sail plan** which needs the minimum of attention. Spinnakers and cruising chutes are not, generally, prudent night-time sails. Some skippers take in a reef in the mainsail and a few rolls in the genoa as a precaution. It depends on the actual and forecast weather, but a slightly shortened foresail will certainly make looking out to leeward a lot easier.

■ *Everyone* on deck must keep a good **lookout**. This is equally applicable by day and is a requirement of the Colregs (Rule 5). Make sure someone ducks down to peer under the foresail at frequent intervals. Also check that a good watch is kept to windward where wind and spray might make this difficult and unpleasant. Fishing gear abounds on both sides of the Channel, and sometimes in the middle, so be prepared to take quick avoiding action if a sharp-eyed lookout spots any. Patches of seaweed often mask other floating hazards such as old rope. Steer round them to be on the safe side.

A good lookout is even more important in a fast power craft, night or day. A submerged object which might cause minor damage to a sailing yacht doing 6 knots could severely cripple, or even sink, a motor cruiser at 20 knots. Similarly, a discarded fishing net or rope round a yacht's propeller may not be a disaster; a single-engine power craft may be totally disabled.

TIP

Children often make excellent lookouts at night. They enjoy the novelty of sailing in the dark and their eyesight is often sharper than those of us of a certain age. However, the younger they are, the more likely they are to fall fast asleep while on watch!

■ Remember that body clocks are at their lowest in the early hours, so keep everyone occupied and ensure a steady supply of **snacks** and **hot drinks**.

■ During quiet periods try to get some **rest** yourself. You are unlikely to drop off into a deep sleep but an hour or so lying down, even in full oilskins, will help to keep you alert for when you are needed.

Fog

Fog is not unusual in the Channel. It is generally well forecast, and you would be unwise to set off if widespread fog was predicted. A report of 'occasional fog patches' in the shipping forecast, on the other hand, is not necessarily a reason to abandon your trip. Sailing in fog is disorientating and somewhat forbidding; you need to be prepared and take appropriate precautions. These include:

■ Put a **fix** on the chart. Fog may envelop you anywhere, but if you are closing land it is essential to refine your position as best you can, and plot it on the chart, before entering an area of poor visibility. Once you are in it, you will have plenty to occupy you.

■ Get **everyone on deck** and looking out. You may wish to send someone to the foredeck where they will not be distracted by others or have the noise of the engine to contend with.

TIP

Brief the lookout to turn towards you before making a report. It is the most natural thing in the world to point (at a ship) and face the same direction!

■ Consider lowering the **spray hood** to give better visibility.

■ **Listen** for big ships' engines: they don't always sound fog signals.

■ If you have **radar**, the most experienced operator should be on constant watch with clear communications to the helm.

■ **AIS** may help identify other ships, but be very cautious about using VHF unless you are absolutely sure you know who you are calling. There may be other small vessels around, and the potential for confusion is enormous. It is far better to obey the Colregs to the letter and do your utmost to avoid any close-quarters situations.

- Wear **lifejackets**, but consider not using harnesses in the cockpit. If you are run down, you don't want to be attached to the boat. For those on deck, the difficulty of recovering an MOB in fog possibly outweighs this risk. It is a judgement call for the skipper.
- Turn on appropriate **navigation lights** and, to comply with the Colregs, make sound signals. They won't be heard in a large ship, but may alert other yachts or fishing vessels to your presence.
- If sailing, be able to **manoeuvre** quickly. Spinnakers and boomed-out headsails should not be used in fog.
- Have the **engine** running, or ready to start, so you can take immediate avoiding action if necessary.
- Have the **liferaft** ready to deploy (take it out of the cockpit locker if that is where it is stowed) with its painter securely lashed to a strong point on the yacht. If you don't carry a liferaft, consider inflating the dinghy and towing it astern.

Colregs for fog

The rules for collision avoidance in poor visibility are very different from those when vessels are in sight of one another. Unlike Rules 11–18, Rule 19 (Conduct of vessels in restricted visibility) makes no distinction between stand-on and give-way vessels; guidance on action to take to avoid collision is quite different, and the usual manoeuvring sound signals do not apply. Rule 19 needs to be read very carefully; parts of it are not immediately obvious, but you really do need to understand it thoroughly. Once you are in fog, you will be far too busy to look it up! In summary:

- **Rule 19(a)** emphasises two points: it applies to vessels which cannot actually see each other, and it is equally applicable when near an area of restricted visibility. In other words, even though you may be in clear visibility, other vessels may be hidden from view in a nearby fog bank. With regard to those ships, you are bound by Rule 19.
- **Rule 19(b)** requires vessels to '... proceed at a safe speed adapted to the prevailing circumstances and conditions...'. A yacht sailing at 6 knots would almost certainly fulfil this requirement; a large container ship doing 25 knots would not. Commercial pressures and the engineering problems of reducing to 'manoeuvring speed' mean that many ships transiting the English Channel do so at a service speed of more than 20 knots, regardless of how far they can see.

In a power craft you will almost certainly need to slow down. One view is that you should be able to stop in half the visibility distance. Contrary to popular belief, this is not in the Colregs, but it's not a bad guide when determining a safe speed.

- **Rule 19(c)** is self-explanatory: you must take into account '... the prevailing circumstances and the conditions of restricted visibility...'. Shipping density, sea state and the effectiveness of your radar are examples of 'prevailing circumstances'.

- **Rule 19(d)** is the key. Subsections (i) and (ii) may seem unnecessarily difficult to interpret, but they boil down quite simply to: always alter your course to starboard to avoid a close-quarters situation unless there is a vessel on your own starboard quarter. In this case you should alter course to port because the rule says you should not alter towards another vessel which is on or abaft your beam.

- The final part, **Rule 19(e)**, is clear: don't take anything for granted, and be ultra-cautious until you are quite sure that no risk of a collision exists.

Unless you are very unlucky, you will not be in fog for long. Focus on the problem; take all necessary precautions; keep a detailed log of your position and alterations of courses and speeds; note any sightings of ships or navigational marks; and breathe a sigh of relief when you pop out into clear visibility.

Opposite: *Other vessels loom out of the fog surprisingly quickly given the short visual range. Keep a good lookout.*

arrival and return

Land was created to provide a place for boats to visit.
Brooks Atkinson

Closing the coast

Having successfully negotiated the Channel shipping lanes and with the open sea behind you, you are now approaching the French coast. Check again how the tidal stream will affect you during the last few hours of the passage. If it is predicted to change direction before you get in, work out the overall set (see Chapter 4) to ensure that you remain comfortably uptide of your destination. If the wind dies you will not then be faced with an 'uphill' struggle to make your entry into harbour.

TELLTALE

Although I never had cause to employ it myself, there was an old navigational 'wrinkle' used by warships before closing a featureless and unfamiliar coast. For a formal visit by an RN ship to a foreign port it is

essential to arrive in some style at a designated point and exactly on time. Faced with a coast of featureless sand dunes (no decent radar echoes) this is no time to crawl in trying to identify the small harbour or anchorage where you are trying to impress the locals.

Before GPS, the routine was to creep along the coast under cover of darkness the previous night. Once the relevant harbour had been positively identified, the ship would clear off over the horizon on a predetermined course for a carefully timed distance. The next day it was simply a matter of running in on the reciprocal course, at high speed, to arrive precisely on time to fire the gun salute.

I can't think of any situation where this might be applicable to a modern yacht, but the principle of identifying your marks before committing yourself to a tricky entrance is as important as ever.

A few years ago we decided to make passage from Guernsey to Alderney passing west of the Casquets to get a good view of the off-lying rocks. Unfortunately, a wind shift and a couple of alterations for shipping put us behind schedule. Having rounded the Casquets, and sailing briskly to the east, we met the full force of the west-going stream and made little progress for several hours. Instead of a sunny afternoon on the beach, we just made it in time for a late supper. My young crew were not pleased. *Mea culpa*.

Keep fixing

In clear visibility you will see the Cotentin Peninsula when you still have several hours left to run. In the excitement of closing a new and unfamiliar coastline it is tempting to abandon your fixing routine. In fact, now is the time to fix more frequently as you start identifying landmarks and getting a feel for the area. Not only do you need to know exactly where you are, you must also determine how the tidal stream is affecting you. It is unlikely to be precisely as shown in the tidal stream atlas. On the return trip, when you first see the high white cliffs of the Isle of Wight, it is easy to think you are nearly home. In fact, you may have another six hours to run!

Opposite top: *Approaching the Casquets from the north*
Opposite bottom: *Enjoying a good meal in Cherbourg*

You do not want to be relying on GPS as you make your final approach: should it fail at this stage you must be sure of your position and have positively identified the marks to help you in. Cherbourg is very straightforward, but many harbours on the north French coast are rather trickier and require careful and precise pilotage. Get as much information as possible from *Reeds* and other pilots or sailing directions. Most people find a sketch in a notebook much easier and quicker to interpret than a list of written notes. Include marks and buoys, your intended track, courses and distances on each leg, and highlight any hazards. You might also note where you plan to lower the sails, call the harbour authority (if required), and prepare warps and fenders etc.

TIP

As with any entry to an unfamiliar harbour, the skipper/navigator should stand back and be free to focus on navigation and oversee the working of the boat. Avoid the temptation to take the helm too early.

Arrival

It is not usually necessary to call the harbour or marina on VHF before you arrive. If you need to, and your French is somewhat rusty, most *capitaineries* (harbour offices) on the Normandy and Brittany coasts have English-speaking staff. In many marinas, including Cherbourg's Port Chantereyne Marina, you will find clearly marked visitors' berths. If you don't, berth anywhere which looks sensible and report to the office as soon as possible. If you are arriving from another EU country it is not normally necessary to produce passports or ship's papers, but you will almost certainly need to complete a short form, the details from which may be entered onto a database, thus reducing paperwork on subsequent visits. A short glossary of useful French words can be found in Chapter 10.

Berthing

There is often a 'welcome' (*accueil*) pontoon where you may go alongside before moving to an assigned berth.

You are probably used to the sort of pontoons found in most UK marinas – substantial, robust and fitted with plenty of decent-sized cleats. French marinas tend

Opposite: *A French catway*

to have short, narrow finger pontoons (*catways*) with hoops rather than cleats. They will almost certainly be significantly shorter than your boat, and you may need to use some ingenuity when rigging lines. Sheet winches and other strong points may have to be pressed into service. Great care is needed when jumping onto a pontoon if you are not to be bounced ignominiously back on board or into the water.

Other berthing options include hammerhead berths at the end of a long pontoon, and alongside/rafting. As at home, it is worth checking when your neighbours are expecting to leave so you can be up and about to lend a hand if necessary.

It is usually a requirement, not restricted to French marinas, to show your receipt for berthing fees in a cabin window. Doing so can prevent an unwelcome awakening by the harbour staff early next morning checking that you have paid.

Getting home

Now that you have arrived after a safe, and hopefully enjoyable, first crossing of the English Channel, you need to get home again. Whatever you do, don't make the all too common mistake of setting out in marginal conditions just because you have to be back by a certain time. Keep an eye on the weather during your stay and leave plenty of time for the return passage; far better to get home early than extend your stay in France until the last minute and be faced with stiff headwinds and a lumpy sea which could have been avoided by sailing a day or two before.

Should the weather deteriorate unexpectedly and you are on a tight schedule, there is no shame in leaving the boat securely alongside and hopping onto a ferry. From somewhere like Cherbourg this poses no difficulties. East of Cherbourg, Calais, Boulogne, Dieppe, Le Havre and Ouistreham are similarly well catered for by frequent ferry services. To the west, there are flights from all of the three main Channel Islands, and ferry services from Guernsey and Jersey. See Chapter 8 for some navigational notes on the more popular ports of departure and arrival on both sides of the English Channel.

Flags and ensigns

Courtesy flags

The discussions on flag etiquette are unending, but there is one rule which, if not followed, may cause grave offence: the proper flying of a courtesy flag. This is a small version of the country's maritime ensign and is hoisted, on its own, at the starboard spreader. In France, a small *Tricolore* should be hoisted when entering

An evening return to the Solent

Courtesy flag

territorial waters (ie, when crossing the 12-mile limit) and left flying until you leave. Foreign vessels visiting the UK should fly the Red Ensign, not the Union Flag (often incorrectly called the Union Jack).

TIP

While we are thinking of flags, the 'order of precedence' in most small craft is: masthead, starboard spreaders, port spreaders. A yacht club burgee should, if possible, be flown at the masthead. However, many mastheads are so cluttered with aerials and wind instruments that it is difficult to hoist a burgee there. In which case, the burgee takes the next position, at the starboard spreader. This poses the question of where to fly a courtesy flag. The answer is to shift the burgee to the port spreader and hoist the courtesy flag in its rightful place at the starboard spreader.

Some traditionalists consider it rather bad form to fly more than one club burgee at the same time. If you have a personal or house flag it should be at the starboard spreader if the burgee is at the masthead, otherwise at the port spreader. However, the golden rule is that a courtesy flag should be on a hoist by itself, not at the top of a string of other flags, nor at the masthead.

Ensigns

This is a good opportunity for a reminder about ensigns. Tradition has it that the ensign should be hoisted at 'Colours' (normally 0800 in the sailing season) and lowered at sunset or 2100, whichever is earlier. Many yachtsmen, possibly most nowadays, tend to ignore this custom and leave the ensign up 24 hours a day while they are living on board. Indeed, some countries require ensigns to be shown at all times so that nationality can be established, day or night.

Do remember that if you belong to a club which is entitled to wear a 'special ensign' – white, blue or defaced red – you *must*, by law, also fly the relevant burgee. The conditions for wearing a special ensign will be printed on your warrant, which must also be on board. It is an offence under the Merchant Shipping Act to wear a special ensign unless you are entitled to do so. Unofficial 'ensigns' – EU flag, or regional flags – are actually illegal (Merchant Shipping Act again) if worn instead of one of the national maritime ensigns.

The ensign is always worn on a staff at the stern or at the peak of a mizzenmast, if fitted. Alternatively, it may be secured to the back stay.

White, blue and red ensigns

pilotage notes

One can advise comfortably from a safe port.
Soren Kierkegaard

To help with the planning process, very brief descriptions of some of the more popular ports, from west to east on both sides of the English Channel, which can be entered at all states of the tide, are shown below. Marinas may not be accessible at all times, but all the harbours listed have either waiting pontoons, visitors' buoys or a suitable anchorage while waiting for the tide. Also included are some notes for departure and entry. Much more detail is shown in *Reeds*, which should always be consulted along with properly corrected official charts.

The position shown after the harbour name is near the entrance. It is for identification purposes only and *must not be used for navigation* unless you have plotted it on a chart and are happy that it is safe and sensible for your needs.

Distances and approximate times to the nearest harbours on the French coast and/or Channel Islands are shown as a guide for planning purposes. They allow for the requirement to cross TSS (and the recommendation to cross the main shipping routes) on a heading at right angles to the general flow of traffic. All the ports shown involve passages of not more than 18 hours based on a speed over the ground (SOG) of 5½ knots.

Motor yachts may, given suitable sea conditions, be able to cover far greater distances in the same timescale. Without wishing to be too obvious, at 15 knots a 60 mile passage will take just four hours; 100 miles will take less than seven hours.

south coast of England

Falmouth (50°08'N 05°02'W)

General: A safe, sheltered harbour with a wide choice of marinas and other moorings and anchorages. The main channels are well marked and lit.

Departure: The harbour entrance is safe in almost any conditions, but may be rough in fresh winds against the ebb tide. Pass either side of Black Rock.

Entry: As for departure. St Anthony Head light has a range of 16 miles; the red sector covers the Manacles Rocks, about 6 miles to the south.

Distance and time: A departure from Helford River (entrance) will reduce this distance by about 3 miles.
Roscoff   97 miles   18 hours

Ashore: An attractive town with good shops and plenty of choice of pubs and restaurants. The National Maritime Museum (Cornwall) is well worth a visit. Miles of river to explore by yacht or dinghy.

Fowey (50°19'.5N 04°38'.5W)

General: A popular yachting harbour with plenty of visitors' buoys and pontoons, but no marinas. Can be uncomfortable in strong south or south-west winds, but may be entered in almost any conditions.

Departure: No particular problems. At night, the white sector of Whitehouse Point light (astern) leads you through the entrance.

Entry: The conspicuous red and white day beacon on Gribbin Head (1.3 miles WSW of the harbour entrance) is a useful mark when approaching from seaward.

Distance and time:

Roscoff	101 miles	18 hours

Ashore: A small town with some good pubs and restaurants. The Royal Fowey Yacht Club welcomes visiting yachtsmen. There are few visitors' berths on the west side of the harbour, so a water taxi or dinghy is necessary to get ashore.

Plymouth (50°19'N 04°10'W)

General: A busy dockyard and ferry port which boasts several large marinas. If making an early start, Cawsand Bay is a good anchorage in moderate westerly winds.

Departure: The main channels are exceptionally well marked and lit. Beware of ships anchored in the Sound, and give warships a wide berth. The Western Channel is a better bet in strong westerly winds, but otherwise the Eastern Channel presents no problems and is usually less busy.

Entry: Although the Western Channel is wider, both channels are deep and well lit. Keep clear of the unlit Shagstone about 1 mile NW of the Mewstone.

Distances and times: Distances are from the breakwater, east or west end.

St Peter Port	89 miles	16 hours
Alderney	90 miles	16 hours
Roscoff	97 miles	18 hours
Trébeurden	100 miles	18 hours

Ashore: Everything a yachtsman could need: pubs, restaurants, chandlers, supermarkets. The Barbican is worth a visit, particularly for arts and crafts – and some of the best fish and chips on the South Coast.

Dartmouth (50°19'·5N 03°33'W)

General: Excellent shelter and easy access, day or night. Visitors' berths may be found in any one of three marinas, alongside on the embankment, on detached pontoons or on buoys.

Departure: The river is well marked and lit. The entrance can be choppy in strong onshore winds.

Entry: The entrance is remarkably difficult to identify from offshore, but the conspicuous daymark on Inner Froward Point, east of the entrance, is a good aiming point when approaching from the south. At night, stay in the white sector of the Kingswear directional light until comfortably north of Dartmouth Castle.

Distances and times:

St Peter Port	71 miles	13 hours
Alderney	72 miles	13 hours
Cherbourg	94 miles	17 hours
St Helier	97 miles	18 hours
Tréguier	99 miles	18 hours
Roscoff	100 miles	18 hours

Ashore: Small but perfectly formed, Dartmouth offers good shops, supermarkets, restaurants and pubs. On the east side of the river, Kingswear is much more limited, but there is a good chandlery, a few pubs and a friendly welcome at the Royal Dart Yacht Club.

Torbay (50°26'N 03°30'W)

General: Brixham and Torquay both provide excellent shelter in well-serviced marinas. In suitable conditions, there are several good anchorages around Torbay, depending on wind direction.

Departure: No problems as the bay is wide open to the east with no off lying dangers.

Entry: As for departure. Follow the fairway in Brixham Harbour to the marina entrance. When approaching the semi-blind entrance to Torquay, keep a sharp lookout for departing vessels.

Distances and times: Distances are from Berry Head. Add 1.5 miles from Brixham, and 4 miles for Torquay.

St Peter Port	73 miles	13 hours
Alderney	72 miles	13 hours
Cherbourg	94 miles	17 hours
St Helier	99 miles	18 hours

Ashore: Although small, Brixham has all the basics, including a couple of supermarkets. Torquay is a very busy tourist town with plenty of nightlife during the summer months. Good beaches and walks.

Weymouth/Portland (50°36'N 05°25'W)

General:

Weymouth can become very crowded in the summer. The marina is above the lifting bridge, but most visitors berth on pontoons either side of the harbour below the bridge. Anchorage in Weymouth Bay NNE of the harbour entrance is feasible in settled weather. Beware of cross-Channel ferries entering and leaving the harbour.

Portland Marina is in the south-west part of Portland Harbour and offers good shelter. In westerly winds there is a safe anchorage in Castle Cove, but the harbour is exposed to winds from the east and north-east.

Departure: Departure from either Portland or Weymouth is straightforward, by day or night. Beware of the three buoys, only one of which is lit, marking the DG range 0.25 miles SE of Weymouth's South Pier Head, and the two noise range buoys, both lit, 1.2 miles SSE of Fort Head. The Shambles Bank, east of Portland Bill, requires careful consideration. Except in calm conditions with a suitable rise of the tide, it is best to pass comfortably to the east or west of the bank.

Entry: Once north of the Shambles, entry to either place poses no particular problems. Entry to Portland for small craft is via the North Ship Channel and the marked fairway to the marina. The South Ship Channel is permanently closed by a blockship with wires between the ends of the breakwaters. Don't even think about it!

Distances and times: Allowing for the transit of Portland Harbour to the North Ship Channel, distances are about the same from either Portland or Weymouth.

Alderney	58 miles	11 hours
Cherbourg	66 miles	12 hours
St Peter Port	76 miles	14 hours
St Vaast	86 miles	16 hours

Ashore: Weymouth is a classic seaside resort with pubs and restaurants to suit all tastes. The splendid sandy beach gets very crowded near the town, but offers a good walk towards the east. Plenty of supermarkets and other shops.

Portland has very few shops within a comfortable walk from the marina, but offers some reasonable pubs. However, close to the marina is a chandler and a good restaurant.

Poole (50°39'N 01°55'W)

General: One of the largest natural harbours in the world, Poole Harbour is generally quite shallow outside the main channels. There are several marinas and good anchorages providing shelter from most directions.

Departure: From the Poole Quay Boat Haven to the Bar Buoy is 4.5 miles and can take well over an hour against the flood stream, which is particularly strong in the narrow entrance. The main channels are well marked and lit, but beware of the large cross-Channel ferries entering and leaving the harbour. The chain ferry between Sandbanks and South Haven Point has right of way over all vessels not carrying a pilot, and it is here that the stream runs particularly hard. Be very careful that you don't get swept onto the ferry or its chains. East Looe Channel, immediately east of the harbour entrance, is shallow but may be used with sufficient rise of the tide, thus avoiding the main Swash Channel which can be quite lumpy with wind against tide.

Entry: As for departure.

Distances and times: Distances are from the harbour entrance. If leaving from Studland Bay subtract 2 miles.

Alderney	60 miles	11 hours
Cherbourg	62 miles	11 hours
St Vaast	78 miles	14 hours
St Peter Port	87 miles	16 hours

Ashore: The old town, near the marina and Town Quay, is very attractive and it is well worth taking some time to explore its history. Not far away is a good supermarket and shopping centre. Plenty of choice for eating and drinking.

Western Solent (50°39'.3N 01°37'.5W – SW Shingles Buoy)

General: The Needles Channel from the Hurst Narrows to the SW Shingles buoy is well marked, by day and night, and can be used in most weather conditions. However, it can be rough in brisk south-west winds when the tide is ebbing, particularly near low water. The North Channel, north of the Shingles, is preferable in strong winds, although Hurst Spit presents a lee shore in southerly winds. During gales, give the whole area a miss and use the eastern entrance to the Solent or make for Poole.

Departure: The tidal streams off Hurst Spit run hard, so a departure on the ebb is recommended. Lymington or Yarmouth may be left at any stage of the tide and in any weather. For an early start consider one of the visitors' buoys outside Yarmouth Harbour. Alternatively, in settled conditions and an offshore wind, a reasonable anchorage may be found NE of Hurst Castle.

Entry: The high white cliffs at High Down are conspicuous from afar, although the Needles lighthouse may not be seen, by day, until much closer in. Beware of the strong cross-tide near The Bridge, particularly if it is setting you on to the Shingles.

Distances and times: Distances are from the Needles lighthouse. Add 6 miles from Yarmouth and 7 miles from Lymington.

Cherbourg	63 miles	12 hours
Alderney	71 miles	13 hours
St Vaast	73 miles	13 hours
St Peter Port	90 miles	16 hours
Le Havre	98 miles	18 hours
Fécamp	98 miles	18 hours

Ashore: Yarmouth is an attractive little town much frequented by visiting yachts. Excellent pubs and restaurants, but rather limited food shops. The Royal Solent Yacht Club is welcoming and provides very good food at reasonable prices.

Across the Solent, Lymington has all you need: chandlers, repair facilities, shops and restaurants. Quay Street, adjacent to the Town Quay, is particularly attractive, and the Saturday market is worth a browse.

Eastern Solent (50°45'N 01°01'W – Horse Sand Fort)

General: A dockyard and ferry port, Portsmouth Harbour provides excellent shelter in several marinas. Yachts, ferries, warships and commercial traffic, coupled with strong tidal streams, can make the narrow entrance lively. However, the harbour may be left or entered in any weather, by day or night.

Departure: Vessels under 20 metres LOA must use the Small Boat Channel (SBC) on the west side of the main approach channel between Ballast Beacon and No.4 Bar Buoy. If leaving on the flood, hug the western side of the SBC where there is often relatively slack water. There can be a very strong set towards the middle of the main channel immediately south of Fort Blockhouse.

Entry: Avoid the worst of the ebb stream by keeping as far to the western side of the SBC as depth allows, but be prepared to alter to starboard for outgoing traffic. Be careful not to stray into the main channel.

Distances and times: Distances are from Horse Sand Fort. Add 3 miles from Portsmouth Harbour entrance, 8.5 miles from Cowes and 11 miles from Hamble River entrance.

St Vaast	76 miles	14 hours
Cherbourg	79 miles	14 hours
Fécamp	88 miles	16 hours
Le Havre	91 miles	16 hours
Alderney	93 miles	17 hours
Ouistreham	95 miles	17 hours

Ashore: The main marinas are on the Gosport side of Portsmouth Harbour where there are some good shops and supermarkets. Eating and drinking opportunities are rather limited compared with Portsmouth which has a far greater choice of restaurants and shops, particularly at Gunwharf Quays which is close to the Portsmouth/Gosport ferry pontoon.

Chichester (50°45'·5N 00°56'·6W)

General: Excellent shelter with six marinas and plenty of space to anchor, although the anchorage off East Head becomes absurdly crowded during summer weekends. The streams run quite hard in the entrance, and the bar (usually dredged to 1.3m) is dangerous in strong southerly winds.

Departure: Some of the channels are not well lit but the southern part of the harbour presents no problem by day or night. Ensure sufficient rise of tide to safely clear the bar. Do not attempt departure in southerly winds of force 6 or above.

Entry: See above. The best time to enter is three hours before to one hour after high water. Later entry, particularly in southerly winds greater than force 5, is not recommended.

Distances and times: Distances are from West Pole Beacon.

St Vaast	75 miles	14 hours
Cherbourg	78 miles	14 hours
Fécamp	87 miles	16 hours
Le Havre	90 miles	16 hours
Alderney	92 miles	17 hours
Ouistreham	94 miles	17 hours

Ashore: The city is a bus ride or long walk from the marina, but the marina itself has a chandlery, a pub/restaurant and a small shop. Chichester Yacht Club is well appointed and friendly. Further down harbour, Itchenor, while attractive, offers few facilities except for the very welcoming Sailing Club and a pub.

Shoreham (50°49'·4N 00°14'·8W)

General: There is total shelter in the East Arm once through the lock. However, the harbour entrance, dredged to 1.9m, can become very rough in strong onshore winds.

Departure: No problems apart from the caution above.

Entry: A radio mast 1000 yards north of the entrance, and a chimney 1200 yards north-east of the entrance, are both conspicuous from seaward.

Distances and times:

Fécamp	69 miles	12 hours
Dieppe	76 miles	14 hours
Boulogne	77 miles	14 hours
Le Havre	83 miles	15 hours
St Vaast	91 miles	16 hours
Calais	91 miles	16 hours
Ouistreham	94 miles	17 hours
Cherbourg	99 miles	18 hours

Ashore: Although Shoreham is a commercial port, it offers good facilities for visiting yachts, including the very friendly Sussex Yacht Club.

Brighton (50°48'·5N 00°06'·4W)

General: The large marina provides good shelter in any weather, but the entrance, dredged to 2m, can be very rough in strong onshore winds.

Departure: No problem given sufficient height of tide for the prevailing conditions.

Entry: As above, but be aware that the only alternative safe harbours are Shoreham (similar limiting conditions in the entrance), 5 miles to the west, and Newhaven, 7 miles east.

Distances and times:

Fécamp	66 miles	12 hours
Dieppe	72 miles	13 hours
Boulogne	73 miles	13 hours
Le Havre	82 miles	15 hours
Calais	86 miles	16 hours
St Vaast	94 miles	17 hours
Ouistreham	94 miles	17 hours

Ashore: All facilities within easy walking distance of the marina berths. Plenty to see and do in the town; a visit to the Royal Pavilion is a must if you have time.

Newhaven (50°46'·3N 00°03·6E)

General: Shelter is good in all weathers but the entrance may become very rough in strong onshore winds. The marina usually has room for visiting yachts.

Departure: Well marked by day and night. The channel is dredged to 6m.

Entry: The best approach is from the south-west, passing 50m off the west breakwater head to avoid heavy seas on the east side of the channel.

Distances and times:

Fécamp	63 miles	11 hours
Boulogne	65 miles	12 hours
Dieppe	67 miles	12 hours
Calais	78 miles	14 hours
Le Havre	82 miles	15 hours
Ouistreham	93 miles	17 hours
St Vaast	97 miles	18 hours

Ashore: A fishing and ferry port, Newhaven has all the usual facilities for yachts, and some good pubs and restaurants. Newhaven Yacht Club is within the marina and welcomes visiting yachtsmen.

Eastbourne (50°47'·3N 00°20·8E)

General: Eastbourne offers excellent shelter in the inner basins via twin locks which are available 24 hours a day. However, the entrance may be rough in strong winds from the south-east. In such conditions, avoid the period 1½ hours either side of high water. The buoyed approach channel is prone to shoaling. If in doubt, check with Sovereign Harbour (VHF or phone). The harbour is somewhat isolated, with Newhaven as the nearest alternative about 12 miles to the west.

Departure: See above. No particular problems but beware of the large wreck, which dries 3m and is marked by two lit green buoys on the north side of the channel.

Entry: By night, a directional light leads into the first part of the channel.

Distances and times:

Boulogne	54 miles	10 hours
Dieppe	62 miles	11 hours
Fécamp	63 miles	11 hours
Calais	64 miles	12 hours
Le Havre	83 miles	15 hours
Ouistreham	96 miles	17 hours

Ashore: Eastbourne itself is some miles from the marina at Sovereign Harbour. However, the marina offers all you need, including a wide range of shops, restaurants and cafés.

Dover (51°06'·6N 01°01'·8E – Western Entrance)

General: Dover is a very busy ferry port. There are strong streams across both entrances, and the harbour is exposed to winds from the NE, through south, to the SW. Shelter is excellent in the marina. If you anchor in the outer harbour, do not leave the boat unattended.

Departure: Once clear of the marina, you must request clearance from Port Control to leave the harbour.

Entry: Obtain clearance to enter, via either entrance, from Port Control. You should make your intentions known when 2 miles off.

Distances and times:

Calais	24 miles	4 hours
Boulogne	28 miles	5 hours
Dieppe	80 miles	14 hours
Fécamp	98 miles	18 hours

Ashore: All facilities, although some may involve a bit of a walk depending on where you are berthed. The Royal Cinque Ports Yacht Club welcomes visiting yachtsmen.

North Brittany coast

L'Aber Wrac'h (48°37'·4N 04°38'·5W)

General: L'Aber Wrac'h is the most westerly all-tide harbour on the north coast of France, and a good jumping-off point for the Chenal du Four and South Brittany. The marina is well sheltered but the visitors' buoys in the river can be uncomfortable in strong NW winds.

Entry: The leading marks are difficult to identify by day, but once you have arrived at the Libenter Buoy there are sufficient marks for safe pilotage.

Ashore: Rather basic facilities, but excellent walks along the riverbank or inland to the supermarket. Some very good local restaurants overlooking the water.

Roscoff (48°43'·5N 03°57'·3W)

General: A new marina has made Roscoff a useful arrival/passage port. The approaches are straightforward and the marina provides good shelter.

Entry: The lighthouse on Île de Batz is conspicuous from afar. No particular problems.

Ashore: A rather pleasant town with reasonable facilities, including a chandlery and several bars and restaurants – all within walking distance of the marina.

Trébeurden (48°46'·3N 03°37'·2W)

General: Although access to the marina is limited by an automatic flap gate over a sill, there are buoys north of Île Milliau and a reasonable anchorage. The latter is exposed to the west.

Entry: From the north, approach west of Les Sept Îles, then pass either west of Le Crapaud reef or, in settled weather and offshore winds, east of the reef to save a few miles. The final approaches are straightforward.

Ashore: Small chandler and basic food shop at the marina. The town, offering a good supermarket and a good choice of places to eat, is close to the marina but uphill!

Channel Islands

Alderney (49°44'·1N 02°11'·2W)

General: Alderney should be avoided in strong winds from the north or north-east when the harbour becomes very uncomfortable. There are about 70 visitors' buoys and plenty of room to anchor, but the range of the tide at springs may make this an unattractive option. No alongside berths, but a marina may be built in a few years' time.

Entry: Beware of the very strong tidal streams running east/west on the final approach from the north. If you miscalculate you will have a long struggle to make up ground. The leading marks keep you clear of the submerged end of the breakwater. The lights are synchronised and easily identifiable by night. Rafting on the buoys is not feasible except in calm, settled conditions.

Ashore: Many good facilities at Bray, including some excellent restaurants. St Anne, the only town, is about a 15-minute walk inland where there are more shops and a supermarket.

St Peter Port (49°27'·4N 02°31'·1W)

General: The capital of Guernsey, St Peter Port may be entered at any stage of the tide and in most weathers but is exposed to the east. The marina, entered over a sill, is well sheltered except from strong easterlies. There are four detached pontoons for visitors and a waiting pontoon for the marina.

Entry: Approach may be made from the north via the Little Russel or the Big Russel. The latter is wider, but the Little Russel is shorter and very well marked by day or night. Beware of high-speed ferries. From the north west, give Les Hanois a wide berth then enter the Little Russel from the south round St Martin's Point. The south coast of Guernsey is relatively free of dangers, but keep well clear of the west coast, particularly in fresh onshore winds.

Ashore: Excellent shopping and many fine pubs and restaurants serving local seafood. Large chandlery next to the fuel berth, about a 10-minute walk from the marina or short dinghy trip when the tide allows.

Normandy coast

Cherbourg (49°40'·5N 01°39'·5W – Passe de l'Ouest)

General: Cherbourg is a large, deep, safe harbour which presents no navigational problems in any weather from any direction. You will normally find a berth on one of several visitors' pontoons in the marina. If not, there is a waiting pontoon, and room to anchor north of the marina breakwater.

Entry: The streams run hard a few miles off but slacken as you approach the harbour. Use either entrance. The Passe de l'Est is rather narrower and used extensively by cross-Channel ferries, but is well marked and lit. Although not prominent, the massive breakwaters become obvious when closer in. Before that, the lighthouse at Pointe de Barfleur, 13 miles to the east, is conspicuous and the chimney at the Jobourg nuclear plant, 10 miles to the west, is also easy to spot. There is plenty of room once inside the Grande Rade to lower sails and prepare for berthing. In poor weather, the Petite Rade offers even more shelter. Do not stray into the charted limits of the military port on the west side of the Petite Rade.

Ashore: Everything you could need, within a few minutes walk from the marina. La Cité de la Mer, a maritime museum which includes the submarine Le Redoubtable, is a short walk from the marina and well worthy visiting. The Liberation Museum, up a long steep hill at Fort du Roule, is also a must when time allows.

St Vaast (49°34'·36N 01°13'·9W)

General: Although the final approaches to the marina dry, there is a good anchorage within about ½ mile of the breakwater, but this is exposed to strong winds from the east and south. The marina, which is accessible 2–3 hours either side of high water, is totally sheltered and there will usually be space for visitors.

Entry: Keep clear of the charted offshore dangers south of Pointe de Barfleur, then exercise some care to correctly identify the various marks and buoys off St Vaast. On your first visit it is wise to leave Le Gavendest Buoy to starboard before heading for the breakwater head and then the marina entrance.

Ashore: A charming town with excellent facilities for visiting yachts. Île Tatihou, accessible by an amphibious craft, has an interesting maritime museum. Bike hire is recommended for a ride out to Barfleur and the lighthouse.

Ouistreham (49°19'·26N 00°14·5W)

General: Ouistreham Marina is entered via the large locks at the start of the canal to Caen. There is a waiting pontoon, which almost dries, outside the locks. The marina itself is completely sheltered but somewhat isolated.

Entry: The approaches are difficult in strong northerly winds, but are well marked by lit buoys and beacons. Watch out for cross-Channel ferries and other commercial ships which have priority over small craft. The locks open about five times each high water.

Ashore: The attractive marina has few facilities and is a longish walk from the town where there a reasonable shops. Caen, 8 miles by canal to the south, is a stunning city boasting excellent shops, restaurants and historic buildings. The marvellous Mémorial Museum is a short bus ride away and worth spending a whole day for a visit.

Le Havre (49°29'·8N 00°02'·3E)

General: A very busy commercial port with a large marina at its western end. The harbour may be entered in any conditions. The approaches are well marked but care is needed to keep clear of large ships, both under way and at anchor. (Honfleur, on the south bank of the Chenal de Rouen, is attractive but navigationally slightly more challenging. It is entered via a lock and adds 8–10 miles to a cross-Channel passage.)

Entry: See above and study *Reeds* and the chart carefully. No real problems except for shipping.

Ashore: A large commercial and ferry port, Le Havre offers all the facilities you could expect from a major town.

Honfleur, on the south side of the Chenal de Rouen, is a delightful picturesque old town with plenty of bars and restaurants. It can become very crowded in the summer months.

Fécamp (49°45'·9N 00°2'1·8E)

General: Although well sheltered in the basins, a considerable surf builds up off the entrance in winds from the west or north-west, and entry is difficult in winds of more than force 5.

Entry: The final approaches and entrance are relatively shallow and prone to silting. However, given reasonable conditions and sufficient rise of tide, and making allowance for cross-currents, entry is straightforward.

Ashore: A very welcoming town with all the usual facilities including good food shops and places to eat. Some excellent walks along the coastal path.

Dieppe (49°56'·3N 01°05'·0W)

General: The marina provides good shelter in all conditions, but northerly winds can cause a heavy swell in the harbour entrance.

Entry: Entry is simple at any stage of the tide, but beware of strong streams across the entrance and commercial traffic. The International Port Traffic Signals (IPTS) must be complied with, both entering and leaving.

Ashore: A very attractive historic town with good facilities for visiting yachts. The various museums are well worth visiting.

Boulogne (50°44'·7N 01°33'·0E)

General: Good shelter in most weathers and at any stage of the tide. Visitors berth on the west side of the river or, for a long stay, in the Bassin Napoléon via a lock. There is a rather exposed anchorage in the north part of the outer harbour.

Entry: The harbour is exposed to the north-west, but entry is straightforward. Having rounded Digue Carnot, steer south to a white mark on the breakwater then towards the inner entrance.

Ashore: Good facilities in the marina, and the town offers plenty of excellent placed to eat, drink and shop. The National Sea Centre (Nausicaa) is a vast aquarium with something to interest all ages.

Calais (50°58'·3N 01°50'·4E)

General: A very busy ferry port with a marina in the completely sheltered Bassin de l'Ouest. The outer approaches require care due to commercial traffic and off-lying sandbanks.

Entry: The entrance itself poses no problems except in strong northerly winds when it can become rough with a heavy swell. You must have your engine running, even if sailing, and obey traffic signals. The lock into the marina is open about two hours either side of high water and there are waiting buoys just outside.

Ashore: Although not particularly attractive, Calais has all the usual facilities you would expect from a reasonably sized town. There is a sandy beach west of the Jetée Ouest.

emergencies

One of the tests of leadership is the ability to recognise a problem before it becomes an emergency.
Arnold H. Glasow

Everything in this chapter applies equally to sailing and motor yachts.

The reason for including a section on emergencies is not because crossing the Channel is particularly hazardous, but because you will be further from help than you are used to when sailing in your local waters, and out of mobile phone coverage for much of the time, so you must have a good working knowledge of emergency procedures to avoid ambiguities, confusion and delays. It is especially important to know the definitions of *Distress* and *Urgency*, as using either in the wrong context may divert expensive and hard-pressed emergency services from more urgent tasks.

Search and Rescue (SAR) in the UK & France

Around the UK the lead authority for SAR is HM Coastguard, which initiates and coordinates all SAR operations, calling on the RNLI, helicopters and any other assets as required. The Coastguard operates from Maritime Rescue Coordination Centres (MRCC) which are shown in Chapter 6 of *Reeds*.

In France, the MRCC equivalent is CROSS (Centres Régionaux de Surveillance et de Sauvetage). CROSS Corsen (north of Brest), CROSS Jobourg (Cherbourg Peninsula) and CROSS Gris-Nez (Cap Gris-Nez to the east) cover the English Channel, and will invariably be able to communicate in English. The French lifeboat service, Société Nationale de Sauvetage en Mer (SNSM), comes under CROSS. SNSM, unlike the RNLI, charges for its services.

Be prepared

Despite the quotation above, emergencies do happen no matter how many precautions you take or how good you are at recognising problems. Mercifully, they tend to be few and far between, but you must be fully conversant with the relevant radio procedures and life-saving signals. It is one of the few requirements for small craft – less than 13.7m/44ft LOA – under Chapter V of the International Convention for Safety of Life at Sea (SOLAS) that *all* vessels have access to a table of life-saving signals. This would be satisfied if you have a copy of *Reeds* onboard. The other requirements are to plan your passage, carry a radar reflector if practicable, report serious hazards to navigation and respond to distress signals.

Equipment

The level of safety equipment carried on board (see Chapter 3) will depend on the size of the vessel, her normal cruising area and the judgement of her skipper. Three items are discussed here:

Mobile telephones have limited coverage (typically no more than about 10 miles offshore); they do not 'broadcast', so other vessels which may be able to help cannot monitor the situation, and they are extremely vulnerable to getting wet. However, if all else fails, a mobile phone may save the day, but don't rely on it.

EPIRBs (**E**mergency **P**osition **I**ndicating **R**adio **B**eacons) and **PLBs** (**P**ersonal **L**ocator **B**eacons) communicate via the Cospas-Sarsat satellite system and may have built-in GPS. They will greatly assist rescue services to find you, particularly if you have been unable to transmit your position beforehand. They cost upwards of £300.

Flares serve two purposes: to raise the alarm and to pinpoint the boat's (or liferaft's) position. Given the cost, limited shelf life and the problems of disposing of them when they reach their expiry date, the viability of flares is becoming questionable, especially now that most yachts carry DSC radios, handheld VHF sets and EPIRBs. A word of caution: the French authorities take a dim view, and may fine you, if they find out-of-date flares on board. If you do carry flares, be sure to read the instructions carefully before you need to use them in anger. They don't all work in the same way, and can cause nasty burns, or worse, if fired incorrectly.

TIP

Even if you do not have red/orange flares in the boat, it is still advisable to have at least a couple of white 'ship scarers' within easy reach of the cockpit. These flares are relatively inexpensive and, used wisely, may prevent you being run down at night by an inattentive large ship. In a sailing yacht, a powerful torch to light up the sails works almost as well.

Definitions

Distress (MAYDAY): A vessel or person is in grave and imminent danger and requires immediate assistance.

The key words are underlined. So unless your situation really is life-threatening and/or you are in danger of losing the boat and you need assistance without delay, you should consider making an Urgency or Routine call.

Urgency (PAN PAN): The calling station has a very urgent message concerning the safety of a ship or person.

An Urgency call may be used, for example, when you need urgent medical advice. It may also be appropriate if you need to alert the Coastguard or other shipping of a serious safety situation which, at the time of the call, falls short of Distress.

You will know the controls on your own radio, but the format for MAYDAY and PAN PAN calls is included here. If you have a DSC radio, follow the instructions for sending the appropriate alert message, but be ready to transmit by voice if an acknowledgement is not received within about 15 seconds.

Distress
MAYDAY MAYDAY MAYDAY

THIS IS (Give the name of your boat three times)

MMSI Number:

Callsign:

MAYDAY (Name of vessel)

MMSI Number (again):

Callsign (again):

MY POSITION IS (Latitude & longitude or true bearing and distance from a known, charted point. If unsure, give a general location such as 'about 10 miles south of the Needles')

Nature of distress (On fire, sinking, dismasted etc)

Number of people on board (It may be helpful to specify adults and children)

Any other important, helpful information (That you are taking to the liferaft, for example)

IMMEDIATE ASSISTANCE REQUIRED

OVER (Wait for a reply. If none received, repeat the message)

Urgency
PAN PAN, PAN PAN, PAN PAN

ALL STATIONS, ALL STATIONS, ALL STATIONS

THIS IS (Give the name of your boat three times)

MMSI Number:

Callsign:

MY POSITION IS (Latitude & longitude or true bearing and distance from a known, charted point. If unsure, give a general location such as 'about 10 miles south of the Needles')

Nature of situation (A safety problem which does not require immediate assistance)

Number of people on board (It may be helpful to specify adults and children)

Any other important, helpful information

Assistance required (if appropriate)

OVER (Wait for a reply. If none received, repeat the message)

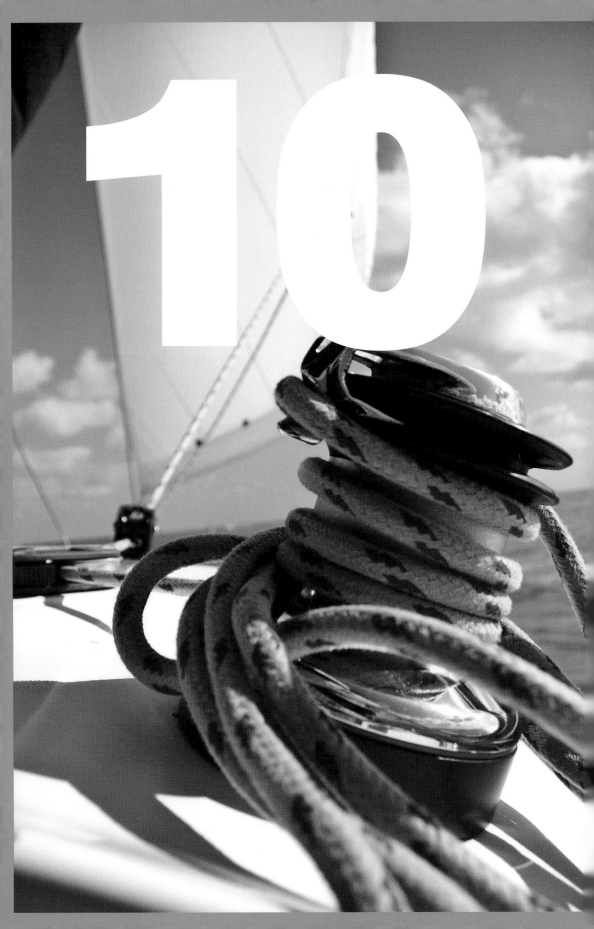

useful French words and phrases

If you talk to a man in a language he understands, that goes to his head. If you talk to him in his language, that goes to his heart.
Nelson Mandela

This chapter lists just a few words which, if your French is as abysmal as mine, you might find useful as you enter harbour and check in at the *capitainerie*. It does not include such basics as *bonjour, merci* or *au revoir*, but may come in handy if, for example, you are asked to produce your *attestation de TVA*.

The staff in most marina and harbour offices on the north coast of France will speak some English, but they will always appreciate an attempt to practise your French, however hesitant. Nelson Mandela got it right.

A more comprehensive vocabulary may be found in the Reference Data chapter of *Reeds*.

English	French
Arrival	L'arrivée
Beam	La largeur
Berthing fees	La taxe d'amarrage
Certificate of competence	Le permis de bateau
Crew list	La liste d'équipage
Customs	La douane
Draught	Le tirant d'eau
Insurance certificate	L'attestation d'assurance
Length overall (LOA)	La longeur
Passport	Le passeport
Port of registry	Le quartier maritime
Ship's papers	Les papiers du bateau/navire
VAT certificate	L'attestation de TVA

Ashore (harbour)	**Le port**
Boat hoist	Le travelift
Boatyard/workshop	Le chantier naval
Chandlery	Le chandler
Crane	La grue
Engineer	Le mécanicien
Fresh water	L'eau potable
Fuel berth	Le ponton de carburant
Harbour guide	Le guide du port
Harbour master	Le capitaine/responsable du port
Harbour/marina office	La capitainerie/le bureau du port
Launderette	La laverie
Mast crane	La grue
Sailmaker	Le voilier
Shower and toilet block	Le bloc sanitaire/les sanitaires
Showers	Les douches
Shower token	Le jeton douche
Toilets	Les toilettes
Yacht club	Le club nautique

English	French
Ashore (town)	**La ville**
Bank	La banque
Chemist	La pharmacie
Dentist	Le dentiste
Doctor	Le médecin
Exchange (money)	Le bureau de change
Hospital	L'hôpital
Post office	La poste
Railway station	La gare
Shop	Le magasin
Supermarket	Le supermarché
Harbour	**Le port/la rade**
Anchoring/anchorage	Le mouillage/l'ancrage
Breakwater	Le brise-lames
Channel (navigation)	Le chenal
Chart	La carte
Cleat	Le taquet
Dinghy (sailing)	Le dériveur
Dinghy (tender)	L'annexe
Dredged (channel)	Dragué
Ferry	Le ferry
Fishing harbour	Le port de pêche
Harbour entrance	L'entrée du port
Hazard	Le danger
Landing place	Le débarcadère
Leading lights	Les feux d'alignement
Lighthouse	Le phare
Lock	L'écluse
Marina/yacht harbour	Le port de plaisance
Mooring buoy	La bouée
Navigational buoy	La balise
Pier	La jetée

English	French
Pontoon	Le ponton
Pontoon, finger	Le catway
Pontoon, long	La panne
Propeller	La hélice
Quay	Le quai
Sea wall	La digue
Slip/slipway	La cale
Wreck	L'épave

Directions	**Les directions**
Abeam	Par le travers
Ahead	En avant
Astern	En arrière
Port (side)	Bâbord
Starboard	Tribord
North	Nord
South	Sud
East	Est
West	Ouest

Navigation	**La navigation**
Chart datum	Zero des cartes
High water	La pleine mer (PM)/La marée haute
Low water	La marée basse
Springs/neaps	Vive-eau (VE)/morte-eau (ME)
Tidal streams	Les courants de marée
Tide tables	Les horaires de marée
Upstream/downstream	En amont/en aval

Weather forecast	**La météo**
Anticyclone	L'anticyclone
Cold front	Le front froid

English	French
Depression	La dépression
Falling (pressure)	En baisse
Fog	Le brouillard
Good (vis)	Bonne
Haze	La brume
Mist	La brume légère
Moderate (vis)	Réduite
Poor (vis)	Mauvaise
Pressure	La pression
Rain	La pluie
Rising (pressure)	Montante
Storm	La tempête
Visibility	La visibilité
Warm front	Le front chaud

Wind	**Le vent**
Beaufort scale	L'echelle de Beaufort
Force 0	Calme
Force 1	Très légère brise
Force 2	Légère brise
Force 3	Petite brise
Force 4	Jolie brise
Force 5	Bonne brise
Force 6	Vent frais
Force 7	Grand frais
Force 8	Coup de vent
Force 9	Fort coup de vent
Gale warning	Avis de coup de vent
Increasing	Augmentant
Moderating	Décroissant

English	French
Sea state	**L'état de la mer**
Calm	Calme
Slight	Peu agitée
Choppy	Agitée
Rough	Forte
Swell	La houle
Emergency	**L'urgence**
Aground (on purpose or accidental)	Echoué
Collision	L'abordage/la collision
Dismasted	Démâté
Distress	La détresse
Help!	Au secours! A l'aide!
Lifeboat	Le canot de sauvetage
Liferaft	Le radeau de sauvetage
Man overboard	Un homme à la mer
Maritime police	La gendarmerie maritime
MRCC (coastguard)	CROSS
RNLI (equivalent)	SNSM
Sinking	En train de couler
The boat is dragging her anchor	Le bateau chasse sur ses ancres
Tow line	Le corde de remorquage

index

Related titles from Adlard Coles Nautical

Your First Atlantic Crossing
4th edition
Les Weatheritt
9780713689495

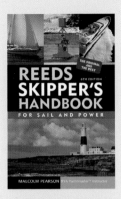

Reeds Skipper's Handbook
6th edition
Malcolm Pearson
9781408124772

First Aid at Sea
6th edition
Douglas Justins & Colin Berry
9781408157039

Instant Weather Forecasting
4th edition
Alan Watts
9781408137093

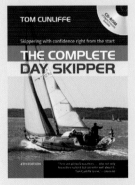

The Complete Day Skipper
4th edition
Tom Cunliffe
9781408178546

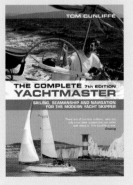

The Complete Yachtmaster
7th edition
Tom Cunliffe
9781408129845

www.adlardcoles.com